Name _____   Date _____

Lesson **1** **Test**

**Find a SYNONYM for each bold word. Then fill in the circle next to your answer.**

1. She **bewailed** the loss of her friend.

   Ⓐ applauded
   Ⓑ regretted
   Ⓒ embraced
   Ⓓ denied

2. The Chief Justice dressed with a touch of **flamboyance.**

   Ⓐ showiness
   Ⓑ tastefulness
   Ⓒ dignity
   Ⓓ brightness

3. Two years of a foreign language seemed an **insuperable** requirement for admission to college.

   Ⓐ reasonable
   Ⓑ silly
   Ⓒ unattainable
   Ⓓ minor

4. The meteorologist predicted **intermittent** rain throughout the weekend.

   Ⓐ periodic
   Ⓑ constant
   Ⓒ unusual
   Ⓓ driving

5. "Early to bed, early to rise" was a **maxim** Connie lived by.

   Ⓐ saying
   Ⓑ cliché
   Ⓒ principle
   Ⓓ advice

**Find an ANTONYM for each bold word. Then fill in the circle next to your answer.**

6. Because Harrison got most of his meals from vending machines, his diet was **destitute** of nutritional value.

   Ⓐ lacking
   Ⓑ without
   Ⓒ needful
   Ⓓ full

7. Hearing that the red team had finished the first leg of the race was an **impetus** to the blue team's efforts.

   Ⓐ obstacle
   Ⓑ credibility
   Ⓒ boost
   Ⓓ energy

8. The anthropologist's documentary series **plumbs** the mysteries of love.

   Ⓐ solves
   Ⓑ ignores
   Ⓒ understands
   Ⓓ examines

9. Rebecca **wheedled** the car from her mother.

   Ⓐ flattered
   Ⓑ coaxed
   Ⓒ gained
   Ⓓ demanded

10. Abolitionist John Brown worked to **emancipate** American slaves.

    Ⓐ liberate
    Ⓑ free
    Ⓒ enslave
    Ⓓ release

**Choose the best way to complete each sentence or answer each question. Then fill in the circle next to your answer.**

11. Members of what profession are most likely to have a **vagabond** lifestyle?

    Ⓐ police
    Ⓑ teachers
    Ⓒ circus performers
    Ⓓ grocers

12. What part of a lake will you reach if you **plumb** it?

    Ⓐ deepest
    Ⓑ warmest
    Ⓒ shallowest
    Ⓓ coldest

13. If someone's talking **detracts** from your enjoyment of a movie, the experience is

    Ⓐ not enjoyable.
    Ⓑ particularly enjoyable.
    Ⓒ less enjoyable.
    Ⓓ more enjoyable.

14. **Destitution** most often refers to people's

    Ⓐ poverty.
    Ⓑ sickness.
    Ⓒ crime.
    Ⓓ hunger.

15. Which group of people will most likely hope for **emancipation?**

    Ⓐ farmers
    Ⓑ foremen
    Ⓒ enslaved people
    Ⓓ laborers

## Standardized Test Preview/Practice

**In this passage, some of the words from this lesson are in bold. Read the passage and then answer the questions.**

Although it is not **obligatory** to help out when natural disasters occur, we are often moved to do something when we watch the news and see families and children who are victims. It is upsetting to see images of people who have lost
5   everything and are **destitute** due to a hurricane, earthquake, or flood. But sometimes being upset urges us to take action.

While most of us can't help directly, we want to be like the hardworking police officers, firefighters, and rescue workers we **extol** for risking their lives in emergency situations. We want
10   to contribute in some way. Fortunately, we can change the sad **visage** of at least one disaster victim into a smiling one by helping support those everyday heroes in our communities and by raising funds for national and international organizations such as the Red Cross.

15   You do not have to **plumb** the depths of your soul to figure out what to do when a natural disaster occurs. Just start by doing something small to help out however you can.

1. In line 1, **obligatory** means
   - Ⓐ important
   - Ⓑ necessary.
   - Ⓒ required.
   - Ⓓ smart.

2. The word **destitute** (line 5) most nearly means
   - Ⓐ having no possessions.
   - Ⓑ having no hope.
   - Ⓒ having no injuries.
   - Ⓓ having an emergency.

3. The meaning of **extol** (line 9) is
   - Ⓐ like.
   - Ⓑ agree with.
   - Ⓒ praise.
   - Ⓓ worry about.

4. In line 11, **visage** means
   - Ⓐ front.
   - Ⓑ surface.
   - Ⓒ mood.
   - Ⓓ hexpression.

5. The phrase "**plumb** the depths of your soul" (line 15) means
   - Ⓐ measure your soul.
   - Ⓑ think hard about.
   - Ⓒ make yourself sad.
   - Ⓓ make your soul vertical.

Name _____ Date _____

**Find a SYNONYM for each bold word. Then fill in the circle next to your answer.**

1. They knew they couldn't go without it, but the hikers felt their bottled water was an **encumbrance** as they headed into the canyon.

   Ⓐ tool

   Ⓑ assistant

   Ⓒ necessity

   Ⓓ burden

2. International aid provided **sustenance** for the families hit hardest by the drought.

   Ⓐ clothing

   Ⓑ transportation

   Ⓒ nourishment

   Ⓓ dessert

3. *Wuthering Heights* is about Heathcliff and Cathy's **torrid** love for each other.

   Ⓐ passionate

   Ⓑ forbidden

   Ⓒ secret

   Ⓓ happy

4. Michele took care to **array** the food on the plates.

   Ⓐ arrange

   Ⓑ toss

   Ⓒ scatter

   Ⓓ scramble

5. The ocean is **fraught** with dangerous creatures.

   Ⓐ scary

   Ⓑ free

   Ⓒ sparse

   Ⓓ full

**Find an ANTONYM for each bold word. Then fill in the circle next to your answer.**

6. T-shirts featuring the mascot were **ubiquitous** at home games.

   Ⓐ common

   Ⓑ everywhere

   Ⓒ rare

   Ⓓ annoying

7. From the dirty plate in the sink, Katie **deduced** that Jim had already eaten dinner.

   Ⓐ guessed

   Ⓑ knew

   Ⓒ reasoned

   Ⓓ figured

8. Clark was always the **laggard** on class field trips.

   Ⓐ demonstrator

   Ⓑ leader

   Ⓒ follower

   Ⓓ slowpoke

9. Bridget's **array** of snapshots was fun to browse.

   Ⓐ display

   Ⓑ design

   Ⓒ order

   Ⓓ mess

10. Inventors rely on their **ingenuity.**

    Ⓐ cleverness

    Ⓑ inventiveness

    Ⓒ training

    Ⓓ stupidity

**Choose the best way to complete each sentence or answer each question. Then fill in the circle next to your answer.**

11. The **zenith** is the spot directly

    Ⓐ above the observer.

    Ⓑ below the observer.

    Ⓒ beside the observer.

    Ⓓ within the observer.

12. To say that something is **inexplicable** means explaining it is

    Ⓐ helpful.

    Ⓑ easy.

    Ⓒ wrong.

    Ⓓ difficult.

13. Which of the following is most likely to **encumber** a cross-country runner?

    Ⓐ wind

    Ⓑ mud

    Ⓒ grass

    Ⓓ shoes

14. Something that is **incontrovertible** cannot be

    Ⓐ questioned.

    Ⓑ proven.

    Ⓒ believed.

    Ⓓ repeated.

15. When people act with **alacrity,** they act

    Ⓐ slowly.

    Ⓑ reluctantly.

    Ⓒ quickly.

    Ⓓ incorrectly.

## Standardized Test Preview/Practice

**In this passage, some of the words from this lesson are in bold. Read the passage and then answer the questions.**

Nyesha was standing in line to buy groceries with her aunt Rachelle when they saw a magazine with the headline "Film Location Revealed." The photo underneath the headline was blurry, as if the picture had been taken from far away, and it

5 showed two celebrities walking toward a car in a **torrid** desert.

"I knew it! They're filming *Spy Me* in the Mojave Desert!" Nyesha's aunt said, snatching the magazine from the rack with **alacrity.**

"Why are you so excited?" Nyesha said, laughing as her

10 aunt peered at the celebrities **arrayed** in desert hiking gear, hats, and sunglasses.

"When I saw them being interviewed on TV, I told your uncle I thought they would film there, and he said no one ever films on location anymore. Ha! He was wrong. Now here's

15 **incontrovertible** evidence that I was right! I'm buying this!"

Nyesha could picture the conversation, her aunt and uncle's voices **fraught** with tension as each tried to prove the other wrong. Somehow, they loved these kinds of arguments. After nearly fifty years together, they enjoyed challenging each

20 other. Nyesha chuckled as her aunt triumphantly slapped the magazine down on the counter to pay for it.

1. In line 5, **torrid** means

  Ⓐ hot and dry.

  Ⓑ passionate.

  Ⓒ fake.

  Ⓓ public.

2. In line 8, **alacrity** most nearly means

  Ⓐ promptness.

  Ⓑ humor.

  Ⓒ eagerness.

  Ⓓ judgment.

3. The meaning of **arrayed** (line 10) is

  Ⓐ grouped.

  Ⓑ collected.

  Ⓒ ordered.

  Ⓓ dressed.

4. The meaning of **incontrovertible** (line 15) is

  Ⓐ unusual.

  Ⓑ visual.

  Ⓒ undeniable.

  Ⓓ understandable.

5. The phrase "**fraught** with tension" (line 17) most nearly means

  Ⓐ full of tension.

  Ⓑ fighting tension.

  Ⓒ scared of tension.

  Ⓓ accompanied by tension.

Name _____     Date _____

**Lesson 3 Test**

**Find a SYNONYM for each bold word. Then fill in the circle next to your answer.**

1. Maria **consecrated** her energies to creating health care for everyone.

   Ⓐ fragmented
   Ⓑ split
   Ⓒ wasted
   Ⓓ devoted

2. My only clue about what was bothering him was the one **allusion** he made to his job.

   Ⓐ reference
   Ⓑ expression
   Ⓒ request
   Ⓓ invitation

3. Speeding in neighborhoods at night without headlights shows a **wanton** disregard for the safety of people who may be walking.

   Ⓐ ignorant
   Ⓑ unaware
   Ⓒ immoral
   Ⓓ accidental

4. The conqueror sought **subjugation** of the conquered.

   Ⓐ liberty
   Ⓑ freedom
   Ⓒ control
   Ⓓ triumph

5. Tasneem **exhorted** her friends not to smoke.

   Ⓐ advised
   Ⓑ requested
   Ⓒ asked
   Ⓓ urged

**Find an ANTONYM for each bold word. Then fill in the circle next to your answer.**

6. Martin's mother worried about her **feckless** son.

   Ⓐ careful
   Ⓑ irresponsible
   Ⓒ lazy
   Ⓓ careless

7. He presented the corsage in a **stilted** manner.

   Ⓐ natural
   Ⓑ artificial
   Ⓒ stiff
   Ⓓ formal

8. The **wanton** kittens found homes quickly.

Ⓐ playful

Ⓑ merry

Ⓒ somber

Ⓓ frolicsome

9. Maureen found that the trick to babysitting was to **dote** on the children.

Ⓐ spoil

Ⓑ deny

Ⓒ pamper

Ⓓ indulge

10. Nathan's **pensive** moods never last long.

Ⓐ thoughtful

Ⓑ active

Ⓒ meditative

Ⓓ reflective

**Choose the best way to complete each sentence or answer each question. Then fill in the circle next to your answer.**

11. Someone **implicated** in a crime is likely to be

Ⓐ victimized.

Ⓑ lying.

Ⓒ judging.

Ⓓ accused.

12. Which of the following least describes **dissemination?**

Ⓐ collecting

Ⓑ scattering

Ⓒ spreading

Ⓓ dispersing

13. "The **trauma** of being orphaned as a child" describes what kind of shock?

Ⓐ physical

Ⓑ moral

Ⓒ emotional

Ⓓ spiritual

14. Which of the following is least likely to be a **lamentation?**

Ⓐ a poem

Ⓑ a song

Ⓒ an essay

Ⓓ a statue

15. **Monetary** is least likely to describe

Ⓐ language.

Ⓑ money.

Ⓒ currency.

Ⓓ coinage.

## Standardized Test Preview/Practice

**In this passage, some of the words from this lesson are in bold. Read the passage and then answer the questions.**

Diana, Princess of Wales, died on August 31, 1997, as the result of a **traumatic** car accident. Her public life as a princess was filled with grandeur, **pomp,** and ceremony, but her private life was known to be troubled. Following her divorce
5 from Prince Charles, she remained beloved by the British people and had millions of fans and followers worldwide. She had a significant impact on the world of fashion and in popular culture that extended beyond her role as a member of royalty. On the day of her funeral, thousands of people
10 lined the streets **lamenting** her sudden death, at age thirty-six, with an incredible outpouring of sorrow. Although tabloid newspapers **alluded** to murder as the reason for her death, it was discovered later that it was nothing but a tragic accident, rather than a **wanton** act of violence.

1. In line 2, **traumatic** means

   Ⓐ horrifying.

   Ⓑ menacing.

   Ⓒ unfortunate.

   Ⓓ emotional.

2. The meaning of **pomp** (line 3) is

   Ⓐ music.

   Ⓑ showy display.

   Ⓒ fine fashion.

   Ⓓ celebrity.

3. The word **lamenting** (line 10) most nearly means

   Ⓐ celebrating.

   Ⓑ talking about.

   Ⓒ feeling grief about.

   Ⓓ singing about.

4. The phrase "**alluded** to" (line 12) means

   Ⓐ hinted at.

   Ⓑ disapproved of.

   Ⓒ rejected.

   Ⓓ proved.

5. The word **wanton** (line 14) most nearly means

   Ⓐ playful.

   Ⓑ deliberate and wrong.

   Ⓒ hidden.

   Ⓓ unfortunate.

Name _____   Date _____

**Lesson 4** **Test**

**Find a SYNONYM for each bold word. Then fill in the circle next to your answer.**

1. Barbara was a **punctilious** host.

   Ⓐ sloppy
   Ⓑ careless
   Ⓒ rude
   Ⓓ attentive

2. Natalie's stories were full of **extraneous** details.

   Ⓐ irrelevant
   Ⓑ important
   Ⓒ necessary
   Ⓓ vital

3. Aunt Edna had an **adage** ready for any occasion.

   Ⓐ fable
   Ⓑ slang
   Ⓒ idiom
   Ⓓ proverb

4. It takes several weeks to **recuperate** from a fractured wrist.

   Ⓐ deteriorate
   Ⓑ weaken
   Ⓒ recover
   Ⓓ submit

5. Insomniacs have to **contend** with many sleepless nights.

   Ⓐ relax
   Ⓑ struggle
   Ⓒ assist
   Ⓓ retreat

**Find an ANTONYM for each bold word. Then fill in the circle next to your answer.**

6. A **sedentary** lifestyle can lead to heart problems.

   Ⓐ lazy
   Ⓑ motionless
   Ⓒ sluggish
   Ⓓ active

7. Sam **regaled** us with stories of his trip to New Zealand.

   Ⓐ bored
   Ⓑ entertained
   Ⓒ delighted
   Ⓓ amused

8. Relations were tense between the best friends in **contention** for the same job.

Ⓐ competition

Ⓑ rivalry

Ⓒ cooperation

Ⓓ tournament

9. Woody preferred to keep his room looking **Spartan.**

Ⓐ luxurious

Ⓑ simple

Ⓒ frugal

Ⓓ restrained

10. His **wry** sense of humor often went unnoticed.

Ⓐ amusing

Ⓑ showy

Ⓒ quiet

Ⓓ understated

**Choose the best way to complete each sentence or answer each question. Then fill in the circle next to your answer.**

11. Which group of people is most likely to enjoy **camaraderie?**

Ⓐ contestants

Ⓑ distant relatives

Ⓒ friends

Ⓓ rivals

12. Which of these things would probably not be among an artist's **paraphernalia?**

Ⓐ matches

Ⓑ paint

Ⓒ canvas

Ⓓ brushes

13. Where are you least likely to find a **hubbub?**

Ⓐ in a library

Ⓑ at a party

Ⓒ at a soccer match

Ⓓ at a pep rally

14. Which of the following is least **odoriferous?**

Ⓐ a rock

Ⓑ a flower

Ⓒ fruit

Ⓓ perfume

15. Which of the following is most likely to **meander?**

Ⓐ a tunnel

Ⓑ a hallway

Ⓒ a stream

Ⓓ an elevator

## Standardized Test Preview/Practice

**In this passage, some of the words from this lesson are in bold. Read the passage and then answer the questions.**

I have a **punctilious** friend named Chao who never displays anything but the most polite manners, no matter where we are or what we are doing. So, what happened one weekend shouldn't have surprised me. We had hiked up a

5  **meandering** trail through the woods that took us to the top of a hill, when Chao stopped. We had been hiking for three hours, and we were sweaty and dirty, with blisters on our feet.

"We need to rest and **recuperate,**" he said. "Would you like something to eat?"

10  "Yes!" I said, grateful as always that Chao was prepared. He reached into his backpack, and I thought he would take out some sort of **Spartan** meal in a plain paper bag, like crackers and peanut butter or trail mix. Instead, with a **wry** smile, Chao pulled out a vinyl tablecloth, napkins, paper plates, salt and

15  pepper packets, hand sanitizer, two individually wrapped turkey sandwiches, and two apples.

"After you," he said after we sat down on a flat rock, waiting for me to take my first bite before he began eating. I had to laugh. There we were, sweating and smelling like

20  insect repellent, yet eating a formal meal on the top of a hill in the woods.

1. The word **punctilious** (line 1) most nearly means
   (A) smart and serious.
   (B) funny and carefree.
   (C) careful and polite.
   (D) friendly and active.

2. In line 5, **meandering** means
   (A) walking.
   (B) winding.
   (C) hiking.
   (D) aimless.

3. The meaning of **recuperate** (line 8) is
   (A) eat a snack.
   (B) start back down.
   (C) regain energy.
   (D) enjoy the view.

4. In line 12, **Spartan** means
   (A) simple.
   (B) heroic.
   (C) fancy.
   (D) nutritious.

5. The meaning of **wry** (line 13) is
   (A) slightly frightened.
   (B) quietly amused.
   (C) fierce.
   (D) wide.

**Lesson 5 Test**

**Find a SYNONYM for each bold word. Then fill in the circle next to your answer.**

1. It was a major undertaking to satisfy the cyclists' **voracious** appetites.

   Ⓐ constant
   Ⓑ anxious
   Ⓒ light
   Ⓓ ravenous

2. **Speculating** in international currency was Mitch's hobby.

   Ⓐ spending
   Ⓑ guessing
   Ⓒ investing
   Ⓓ profiting

3. There are many **impediments** to earning a college degree.

   Ⓐ obstacles
   Ⓑ bridges
   Ⓒ distractions
   Ⓓ dangers

4. Joseph Stalin was a Soviet **despot** who was responsible for the deaths of millions.

   Ⓐ benefactor
   Ⓑ tyrant
   Ⓒ patron
   Ⓓ pushover

5. Ms. Perera can always be counted on to give **sagacious** advice.

   Ⓐ absurd
   Ⓑ reckless
   Ⓒ foolish
   Ⓓ wise

**Find an ANTONYM for each bold word. Then fill in the circle next to your answer.**

6. Her **indolence** affected her ability to keep a job.

   Ⓐ dedication
   Ⓑ inefficiency
   Ⓒ idleness
   Ⓓ drowsiness

7. Politics had been a source of **strife** at the dinner table on countless holidays.

   Ⓐ boredom
   Ⓑ struggle
   Ⓒ fighting
   Ⓓ harmony

8. Rising property taxes threatened to **impoverish** the new homeowner.

 Ⓐ diminish

 Ⓑ worry

 Ⓒ enrich

 Ⓓ hinder

9. Andy made a point to **enunciate** his words.

 Ⓐ mumble

 Ⓑ pronounce

 Ⓒ sing

 Ⓓ project

10. Most state holidays are **secular.**

 Ⓐ religious

 Ⓑ commonplace

 Ⓒ worldly

 Ⓓ mundane

**Choose the best way to complete each sentence or answer each question. Then fill in the circle next to your answer.**

11. Crops in **impoverished** soil are most likely to

 Ⓐ grow.

 Ⓑ die.

 Ⓒ blossom.

 Ⓓ thrive.

12. To **venerate** something means to treat it with

 Ⓐ respect.

 Ⓑ contempt.

 Ⓒ fondness.

 Ⓓ sympathy.

13. A **cynic** is not

 Ⓐ suspicious.

 Ⓑ doubtful.

 Ⓒ skeptical.

 Ⓓ trusting.

14. **Contemporaries** are of the same

 Ⓐ country.

 Ⓑ ingredients.

 Ⓒ time.

 Ⓓ magnitude.

15. Someone who is **callow** is not likely to be

 Ⓐ skilled.

 Ⓑ young.

 Ⓒ new.

 Ⓓ inexperienced.

## Standardized Test Preview/Practice

**In this passage, some of the words from this lesson are in bold. Read the passage and then answer the questions.**

Ideas about how older people should be treated, and what their characteristics are, vary depending on culture. In many cultures, the elderly are seen as **sagacious** due to a lifetime of experience and lessons learned, and are therefore

5 worthy of the utmost respect. It is taken for granted that adult children will take care of their parents once the parents become elderly, regarding such care as an honor and privilege. Those who don't do this are seen as lazy and **indolent.**

In other cultures, however, it is more common for the

10 elderly to live alone or to spend their last days in a nursing home and to be seen as mentally fragile. Some take an even more **cynical** view, believing that the elderly are purposely irritating and intrude too often in younger people's lives. They doubt older people's intentions when they offer advice.

15 If you grew up thinking that older people don't have something to offer, it's important to question this attitude. It is **callow** and foolish to assume that you know more than someone who is older than you. Those with a **voracious** desire to learn, especially about history, should consider how much

20 experience an elderly person has, and what knowledge and wisdom he or she might share.

1. In line 3, **sagacious** means

   Ⓐ wise.

   Ⓑ respected.

   Ⓒ experienced.

   Ⓓ capable.

2. The word **indolent** (line 8) most nearly means

   Ⓐ disrespectful.

   Ⓑ avoiding work.

   Ⓒ dishonorable.

   Ⓓ unreliable.

3. In line 12, **cynical** most nearly means

   Ⓐ wise.

   Ⓑ realistic.

   Ⓒ skeptical.

   Ⓓ unfair.

4. The meaning of **callow** (line 17) is

   Ⓐ mean.

   Ⓑ stupid.

   Ⓒ bold.

   Ⓓ immature.

5. In line 18, **voracious** means

   Ⓐ hungry.

   Ⓑ eager.

   Ⓒ small.

   Ⓓ sufficient.

Name _____  Date _____

**Find a SYNONYM for each bold word. Then fill in the circle next to your answer.**

1. After debating for an hour, Marla **conceded** John's point that education was a benefit.

   Ⓐ denied
   Ⓑ admitted
   Ⓒ insisted
   Ⓓ argued

2. Jim is **dogmatic** about the benefits of a low-protein diet.

   Ⓐ assertive
   Ⓑ timid
   Ⓒ unsure
   Ⓓ open-minded

3. The witness was asked to **aver** that she had seen a third person at the holdup.

   Ⓐ ask
   Ⓑ declare
   Ⓒ wonder
   Ⓓ mislead

4. The menu at the vegetarian restaurant **embodies** the chef's beliefs about good nutrition.

   Ⓐ incorporates
   Ⓑ represents
   Ⓒ visualizes
   Ⓓ splinters

5. Callie refused to be a part of the **propagation** of rumors.

   Ⓐ absence
   Ⓑ shortage
   Ⓒ abundance
   Ⓓ spread

**Find an ANTONYM for each bold word. Then fill in the circle next to your answer.**

6. "Stretch" was an **apropos** nickname for the lanky runner.

   Ⓐ apt
   Ⓑ inappropriate
   Ⓒ suitable
   Ⓓ fitting

7. The demise of the newsreel coincided with the **ascendancy** of network television news.

   Ⓐ control
   Ⓑ power
   Ⓒ decline
   Ⓓ superiority

8. Mom **imparted** basic cooking abilities to all her children.

Ⓐ disclosed

Ⓑ revealed

Ⓒ withheld

Ⓓ gave

9. Concerned parents organized a book drive to address the **deficiency** of books in the library.

Ⓐ lack

Ⓑ excess

Ⓒ shortage

Ⓓ need

10. Students were asked to prepare **rudimentary** outlines of their projects the next day.

Ⓐ complete

Ⓑ elementary

Ⓒ simple

Ⓓ initial

**Choose the best way to complete each sentence or answer each question. Then fill in the circle next to your answer.**

11. Which professional has the least need for **oratory?**

Ⓐ politician

Ⓑ actor

Ⓒ programmer

Ⓓ general

12. Which of the following is furthest from the definition of **assess?**

Ⓐ determine

Ⓑ judge

Ⓒ share

Ⓓ estimate

13. Which business does not rely upon making something **propagate?**

Ⓐ music

Ⓑ gardening

Ⓒ farming

Ⓓ breeding

14. A person who is **deficient** in something has

Ⓐ enough of it.

Ⓑ not enough of it.

Ⓒ too much of it.

Ⓓ an excess of it.

15. To **sojourn** refers to

Ⓐ staying somewhere.

Ⓑ enjoying something.

Ⓒ traveling.

Ⓓ shopping.

## Standardized Test Preview/Practice

**In this passage, some of the words from this lesson are in bold. Read the passage and then answer the questions.**

The most amazing thing happened the other day in debate club. We were having a practice debate about school uniforms when things got a little heated. DeShawn, the president of the debate club, yelled, "UNIFORMS SHOULD BE
5   ILLEGAL!" three times in a row, while the girl he was debating, who had just joined the club, sat there quietly with her arms crossed. After a long silence, she said, "In my **assessment,** your **oratorical** skills are lacking. You're not arguing effectively. You're just **vociferous.** Shouting the same thing over and over
10  again is not going to convince anyone of anything."

First, DeShawn looked angry, then he looked embarrassed, and, finally, he looked defeated. He slumped back in his chair and nodded slowly.

"I have to **concede** that you are right," he said as the whole
15  room watched in silence. Then he stood up ceremoniously, cleared his throat, and announced, "So, this is the end of my **sojourn** as a member of this debate club. I quit!" Then he walked out. We were all stunned. No one knew what to do. Then my friend tapped the new girl on the shoulder and asked
20  her if *she* wanted to be the president of the debate club.

1. The meaning of **assessment** (line 7) is

   Ⓐ test.
   Ⓑ carefully considered opinion.
   Ⓒ mind.
   Ⓓ heart.

2. In line 7, **oratorical** means

   Ⓐ speaking.
   Ⓑ personal.
   Ⓒ academic.
   Ⓓ leadership.

3. The word **vociferous** (line 9) most nearly means

   Ⓐ rude.
   Ⓑ stupid.
   Ⓒ loud.
   Ⓓ arrogant.

4. In line 14, **concede** means

   Ⓐ say.
   Ⓑ admit.
   Ⓒ explain.
   Ⓓ deny.

5. The meaning of **sojourn** (line 17) is

   Ⓐ journey.
   Ⓑ time.
   Ⓒ visit.
   Ⓓ trip.

Name _____    Date _____

**Find a SYNONYM for each bold word. Then fill in the circle next to your answer.**

1. Lisa became more **voluble** as she got more excited.

   Ⓐ loud
   Ⓑ chatty
   Ⓒ shy
   Ⓓ reserved

2. Marcus **deemed** it necessary to spend all weekend preparing his presentation.

   Ⓐ suspected
   Ⓑ imagined
   Ⓒ doubted
   Ⓓ considered

3. You can collect **exorbitant** fees for doing something everyone needs done but no one wants to do.

   Ⓐ excessive
   Ⓑ reasonable
   Ⓒ inexpensive
   Ⓓ expected

4. The organization offered a **subsidy** to researchers willing to study pond scum.

   Ⓐ loan
   Ⓑ plan
   Ⓒ license
   Ⓓ grant

5. Yvette **belittled** her contribution to the success of the project.

   Ⓐ minimized
   Ⓑ complimented
   Ⓒ flattered
   Ⓓ inflated

**Find an ANTONYM for each bold word. Then fill in the circle next to your answer.**

6. Paul expected a **censure** for being out past curfew.

   Ⓐ approval
   Ⓑ disapproval
   Ⓒ criticism
   Ⓓ judgment

7. The tree is **moribund.**

   Ⓐ growing
   Ⓑ dying
   Ⓒ ailing
   Ⓓ falling

8. Alex was uncomfortable seeing **amorous** displays in public.

   Ⓐ friendly
   Ⓑ romantic
   Ⓒ fickle
   Ⓓ hateful

9. He used his bonus to treat his parents to a **sumptuous** dinner.

   Ⓐ luxurious
   Ⓑ extravagant
   Ⓒ expensive
   Ⓓ meager

10. Unfortunately, Greg is likely to **divulge** other people's secrets.

    Ⓐ reveal
    Ⓑ conceal
    Ⓒ disclose
    Ⓓ tell

**Choose the best way to complete each sentence or answer each question. Then fill in the circle next to your answer.**

11. Who is most likely to issue an **injunction** prohibiting something?

    Ⓐ a judge
    Ⓑ a boss
    Ⓒ a friend
    Ⓓ a principal

12. **Fateful** refers to something's

    Ⓐ consequences.
    Ⓑ validity.
    Ⓒ truth.
    Ⓓ luck.

13. An **ingrate** lacks

    Ⓐ attitude.
    Ⓑ gratitude.
    Ⓒ manners.
    Ⓓ friends.

14. In which class are you most likely to study a **motif?**

    Ⓐ history
    Ⓑ math
    Ⓒ literature
    Ⓓ science

15. To **expostulate** is to attempt to

    Ⓐ denounce.
    Ⓑ convince.
    Ⓒ dissuade.
    Ⓓ dominate.

## Standardized Test Preview/Practice

**In this passage, some of the words from this lesson are in bold. Read the passage and then answer the questions.**

"How could you **divulge** my secret to everyone?" Afshan asked the minute I sat down next to her at lunch.

"What are you talking about?" I replied, trying hard to remember any secrets she might have shared with me.

5 "*You* know," she said.

I frowned. What had she told me that could be **deemed** a secret? The usually **voluble** Afshan sat there silently, her arms crossed under her irate visage. Finally something clicked in my apparently **moribund** brain cells.

10 "Oh! You mean telling Mina and Devere that you're trying out for the track team?"

Afshan said nothing and nodded angrily, biting into her sandwich.

"I didn't know you were keeping that a secret," I said. "I
15 thought you would want your best friends to know so they could wish you good luck." Afshan's face softened a little. I handed her my apple and banana. "I saved these for you," I said.

Afshan rolled her eyes, but I also saw her start to smile.

**"Ingrate!"** I said, laughing. "You didn't even thank me for
20 providing healthy snacks so you'll have energy to try out for the team!"

Finally, Afshan laughed, and I knew I was forgiven. What a relief!

1. The word **divulge** (line 1) most nearly means

Ⓐ reveal.

Ⓑ shout.

Ⓒ explain.

Ⓓ describe.

2. The meaning of **deemed** (line 6) is

Ⓐ made.

Ⓑ revealed as.

Ⓒ considered.

Ⓓ presented as.

3. In line 7, **voluble** most nearly means

Ⓐ nice

Ⓑ talkative.

Ⓒ friendly.

Ⓓ sympathetic.

4. In line 9, **moribund** means

Ⓐ nonexistent.

Ⓑ hard-working.

Ⓒ energized.

Ⓓ dying.

5. The word **ingrate** (line 19) most nearly means

Ⓐ unkind person.

Ⓑ enemy.

Ⓒ ungrateful person.

Ⓓ friend.

Name _____ Date _____

**Find a SYNONYM for each bold word. Then fill in the circle next to your answer.**

1. Marilyn's **demeanor** was affected by years in prison.

   Ⓐ appearance

   Ⓑ outfit

   Ⓒ behavior

   Ⓓ expression

2. It is easier to renew your license than to let it **lapse** and get it reinstated.

   Ⓐ expire

   Ⓑ slip

   Ⓒ disappear

   Ⓓ continue

3. The Food and Drug Administration is the **definitive** authority on nutrition.

   Ⓐ initial

   Ⓑ likely

   Ⓒ possible

   Ⓓ final

4. Be careful not to **affront** your elders with offensive jokes.

   Ⓐ insult

   Ⓑ flatter

   Ⓒ inform

   Ⓓ suggest

5. Barry's habit of gossiping made him a **pariah** to those he talked about.

   Ⓐ enemy

   Ⓑ outcast

   Ⓒ insider

   Ⓓ friend

**Find an ANTONYM for each bold word. Then fill in the circle next to your answer.**

6. The five minutes after the last bell on the last day of school were the most **raucous** the school had known all year.

   Ⓐ boisterous

   Ⓑ serene

   Ⓒ noisy

   Ⓓ disorderly

7. When not studying or spending time with friends, Pat enjoyed his **avocation** of collecting first-edition books.

   Ⓐ hobby

   Ⓑ career

   Ⓒ pastime

   Ⓓ investment

8. It helps to be **erudite** in many topics to win trivia contests.

   Ⓐ ignorant
   Ⓑ learned
   Ⓒ knowledgeable
   Ⓓ smart

9. Carolyn enjoyed guiding her **protégé.**

   Ⓐ accomplice
   Ⓑ peer
   Ⓒ student
   Ⓓ mentor

10. Her **adroit** handling of the race car made it look easy.

   Ⓐ clumsy
   Ⓑ skillful
   Ⓒ clever
   Ⓓ adept

**Choose the best way to complete each sentence or answer each question. Then fill in the circle next to your answer.**

11. A **militant** is one who is ready to

   Ⓐ debate.
   Ⓑ picket.
   Ⓒ negotiate.
   Ⓓ fight.

12. A **lapse** in memory will cause you to

   Ⓐ think.
   Ⓑ lie.
   Ⓒ forget.
   Ⓓ remember.

13. Who is most likely to be **inducted?**

   Ⓐ a president
   Ⓑ a mechanic
   Ⓒ a gardener
   Ⓓ a secretary

14. Which of the following best describes something that is **tacit?**

   Ⓐ communicated
   Ⓑ spoken
   Ⓒ implied
   Ⓓ expressed

15. Which word does not describe **crusading?**

   Ⓐ passionate
   Ⓑ easy
   Ⓒ struggling
   Ⓓ prolonged

## Standardized Test Preview/Practice

In this passage, some of the words from this lesson are in bold. Read the passage and then answer the questions.

My little brother Javier can be hard to handle when he has to be quiet or keep still. We were at a classical-music concert when a six-year-old violin **prodigy** was introduced. As he started playing, Javier stood up, pointed at him, and said
5  loudly, "He's the same age as me!" The audience laughed, but it was such bad timing! I was so embarrassed. Meanwhile, Mami gave him her **tacit** approval by smiling as she shushed him.

The whole situation reminded me of my National Honor Society **induction** ceremony, when Javier had yelled, "THAT'S
10  MY SISTER!" just as I was welcomed into the society by accepting a gold pin from my school's principal. Javier just doesn't understand that being **raucous** at formal events isn't acceptable.

If he doesn't learn soon when to keep quiet, I am not sure
15  what I will do. Mami says he's only six and will learn how to control himself better when he gets older. I hope so, because I don't want to be at my high school or college graduation ceremony and have him **lapse** into behavior that makes me cringe and turn red with embarrassment.

1. The meaning of **prodigy** (line 3) is

  Ⓐ highly accomplished musician.

  Ⓑ student with serious intentions.

  Ⓒ young person with extraordinary talent.

  Ⓓ academic genius.

2. The word **tacit** (line 7) most nearly means

  Ⓐ warm.

  Ⓑ motherly.

  Ⓒ silent.

  Ⓓ clear.

3. The meaning of **induction** (line 9) is

  Ⓐ final.

  Ⓑ award.

  Ⓒ graduation.

  Ⓓ introduction.

4. In line 12, **raucous** most nearly means

  Ⓐ rude and malicious.

  Ⓑ disruptive and loud.

  Ⓒ energetic.

  Ⓓ expressive.

5. The phrase "**lapse** into" (line 18) means

  Ⓐ slip back into.

  Ⓑ blend into.

  Ⓒ change into.

  Ⓓ look into.

Name _____ Date _____

Lesson **9** **Test**

**Find a SYNONYM for each bold word. Then fill in the circle next to your answer.**

1. Radiocarbon dating is used to establish the **antiquity** of artifacts.

   Ⓐ value
   Ⓑ beauty
   Ⓒ demand
   Ⓓ age

2. The teammates **appraised** each other's performances.

   Ⓐ evaluated
   Ⓑ admired
   Ⓒ polished
   Ⓓ studied

3. The neighbors **reposed** their trust in small claims court to decide who was responsible for the fence.

   Ⓐ withheld
   Ⓑ placed
   Ⓒ removed
   Ⓓ lost

4. Dan used his biggest knife to **cleave** the watermelon into halves.

   Ⓐ split
   Ⓑ mend
   Ⓒ shatter
   Ⓓ merge

5. Roger had a hard time identifying his **nondescript** umbrella in the lost-and-found.

   Ⓐ ornate
   Ⓑ unusual
   Ⓒ flamboyant
   Ⓓ plain

**Find an ANTONYM for each bold word. Then fill in the circle next to your answer.**

6. Daria took care with her guest list to make sure conversation at her dinner parties was always **scintillating.**

   Ⓐ animated
   Ⓑ lively
   Ⓒ brilliant
   Ⓓ dull

7. Detectives **scrutinized** the accident scene before preparing their report.

   Ⓐ examined
   Ⓑ glimpsed
   Ⓒ investigated
   Ⓓ inspected

8. Music purists **depreciate** new fusion styles.

Ⓐ endorse

Ⓑ belittle

Ⓒ disparage

Ⓓ insult

9. **Synthetic** fabrics offer both advantages and disadvantages over cotton and wool.

Ⓐ artificial

Ⓑ shiny

Ⓒ fake

Ⓓ natural

10. A **facsimile** of the signed contract was all the banker needed to begin processing the loan.

Ⓐ forgery

Ⓑ original

Ⓒ replica

Ⓓ copy

**Choose the best way to complete each sentence or answer each question. Then fill in the circle next to your answer.**

11. **Allure** refers to the power to

Ⓐ trap.

Ⓑ deceive.

Ⓒ attract.

Ⓓ repel.

12. **Transmuting** is most closely related to

Ⓐ balancing.

Ⓑ creating.

Ⓒ changing.

Ⓓ maintaining.

13. Which of the following is most likely to have **facets?**

Ⓐ an emerald

Ⓑ a pearl

Ⓒ a band

Ⓓ a nugget

14. If something is **impervious,** it is

Ⓐ vulnerable.

Ⓑ unaffected.

Ⓒ disrupted.

Ⓓ penetrated.

15. Which of the following does not describe a **quandary?**

Ⓐ uncertainty

Ⓑ doubt

Ⓒ puzzlement

Ⓓ confidence

## Standardized Test Preview/Practice

**In this passage, some of the words from this lesson are in bold. Read the passage and then answer the questions.**

What do you picture when you hear the word *suburb?* Many people imagine rows of **nondescript,** boxlike houses, each a **facsimile** of the others. They imagine that the people living in the houses are all the same, too. It might be easy

5 to make such an assumption from the outside. They can't see beyond the sameness of the houses to realize that the individuals inside are different and distinctive.

Residents of houses in the suburbs, however, know just how unique they are, and how unique their communities are.

10 Over time, as they make connections with friends and family within those communities, they become **impervious** to the judgment from outsiders. They know they don't have to make a choice between **reposing** in a quiet suburban backyard and having **scintillating** conversations with fascinating

15 people—they can have both. A good conversation can happen anywhere!

1. In line 2, **nondescript** means
   Ⓐ indescribable.
   Ⓑ unremarkable.
   Ⓒ beyond description.
   Ⓓ distinctive.

2. The meaning of **facsimile** (line 3) is
   Ⓐ exact copy.
   Ⓑ different version.
   Ⓒ a part.
   Ⓓ a detail.

3. In line 11, **impervious** most nearly means
   Ⓐ not penetrable.
   Ⓑ concerned by.
   Ⓒ not affected by.
   Ⓓ affected by.

4. The word **reposing** (line 13) most nearly means
   Ⓐ lying down.
   Ⓑ resting and relaxing.
   Ⓒ placing power in.
   Ⓓ sleeping.

5. In line 14, **scintillating** means
   Ⓐ flashing.
   Ⓑ sparkling.
   Ⓒ lively.
   Ⓓ intellectual.

Name _____  Date _____

**Lesson 10  Test**

**Find a SYNONYM for each bold word. Then fill in the circle next to your answer.**

1. Tuition at certain state schools is **gratis** to military veterans.

   Ⓐ conditional
   Ⓑ costly
   Ⓒ free
   Ⓓ restricted

2. Volunteers donate their time without expecting to be **remunerated.**

   Ⓐ paid
   Ⓑ billed
   Ⓒ charged
   Ⓓ gifted

3. The community will be the **beneficiary** of the money for the botanical gardens.

   Ⓐ manager
   Ⓑ patron
   Ⓒ donor
   Ⓓ receiver

4. The community center **solicited** canned goods for the food bank.

   Ⓐ requested
   Ⓑ denied
   Ⓒ endorsed
   Ⓓ lured

5. Since none of them won the competition, the class **commiserated** together.

   Ⓐ celebrated
   Ⓑ sympathized
   Ⓒ distracted
   Ⓓ gloated

**Find an ANTONYM for each bold word. Then fill in the circle next to your answer.**

6. The choral group **garnered** several rave reviews at the state competition.

   Ⓐ collected
   Ⓑ distributed
   Ⓒ gathered
   Ⓓ earned

7. The paper recycling campaign had been Mr. Horowitz's pet project since its **inception.**

   Ⓐ start
   Ⓑ middle
   Ⓒ end
   Ⓓ duration

8. The surgeon had to **amputate** Mel's fingertip to save his hand.

   Ⓐ sever
   Ⓑ remove
   Ⓒ reattach
   Ⓓ bandage

9. Howie felt **magnanimous** as long as there was money in his pocket.

   Ⓐ selfish
   Ⓑ generous
   Ⓒ giving
   Ⓓ kind

10. The bureau blocked a **practicable** exit.

   Ⓐ useable
   Ⓑ useless
   Ⓒ functional
   Ⓓ ornamental

**Choose the best way to complete each sentence or answer each question. Then fill in the circle next to your answer.**

11. Friends told her "all things happen for a reason" so often during her ordeal that the sentiment became **trite.** What best describes the sentiment?

   Ⓐ fresh
   Ⓑ new
   Ⓒ overused
   Ⓓ original

12. There are **myriads** of fish in the sea. Which of the following best describes the fish?

   Ⓐ scarce
   Ⓑ abundant
   Ⓒ rare
   Ⓓ extinct

13. Which of the following is most likely to be **amputated?**

   Ⓐ appendix
   Ⓑ tonsils
   Ⓒ tooth
   Ⓓ toe

14. Which does not describe an **aptitude?**

   Ⓐ talent
   Ⓑ ability
   Ⓒ challenge
   Ⓓ gift

15. Which of the following is true of a **boon?** It is

   Ⓐ welcome.
   Ⓑ unwanted.
   Ⓒ inconvenient.
   Ⓓ dreaded.

## Standardized Test Preview/Practice

In this passage, some of the words from this lesson are in bold. Read the passage and then answer the questions.

The United States government does not financially support its Olympic athletes. In many other countries around the world, athletes with enormous **aptitude** are identified at an early age. They then receive financial backing from the
5  government to ensure they are trained to realize their greatest potential.

Unfortunately, for many U.S. athletes, the most difficult obstacle in the path to victory at the Olympics isn't skill, effort, or talent—it's their **incapacity** to raise the funds
10  needed to continue full-time training. Athletes who are able to successfully **solicit** funding for their athletic careers from **magnanimous** donors have their basic costs covered, but these athletes are rarely wealthy. After all, Olympians aren't **remunerated** for the hours they spend training. Only the most
15  famous U.S. Olympic athletes are sponsored by companies and therefore paid the way we might expect, given their talent and status.

1. The meaning of **aptitude** (line 3) is

   Ⓐ muscles.

   Ⓑ careers.

   Ⓒ fitness.

   Ⓓ talent.

2. In line 9, **incapacity** means

   Ⓐ decision.

   Ⓑ inability.

   Ⓒ necessity.

   Ⓓ mission.

3. The word **solicit** (line 11) most nearly means

   Ⓐ start.

   Ⓑ expand.

   Ⓒ get from others.

   Ⓓ increase.

4. In line 12, **magnanimous** means

   Ⓐ wealthy.

   Ⓑ invested.

   Ⓒ generous.

   Ⓓ encouraging.

5. In line 14, the phrase "**remunerated** for" means

   Ⓐ paid for.

   Ⓑ celebrated for.

   Ⓒ honored for.

   Ⓓ understood for.

Name _____ Date _____

Read the passage. Choose the best answer for each sentence or question about a bold word. Then fill in the circle next to your answer.

## Absolute Power Corrupts Absolutely

How did Maximilien Robespierre, a country lawyer devoted to protecting the oppressed and **impoverished,** come to **embody** the horror of the darkest days of the French Revolution? As a young lawyer in his hometown of Arras, he sought to "pursue with vengeful words those who, without pity for humanity, enjoy the suffering of others." While serving as a judge in 1782, he was **incapacitated** with despair at having to pronounce a death sentence. He found the responsibility of ending a person's life so **traumatic** that he resigned his position as a judge and returned to his law practice.

He was known to his **contemporaries** as "the Incorruptible." While he was known to be moral and honest, he was certainly not humble. He published pamphlets about his successes in the courtroom to enhance his reputation and **disseminate** news of his triumphs.

In 1789, the king called a meeting of the Estates-General to hear the people's complaints, and Robespierre was sent to represent his province at the meeting. A Paris mob soon stormed the Bastille, a prison where people were jailed for their political beliefs. The Revolution was underway.

Robespierre wanted a new government and spent the next few years making speeches calling for the king's execution. His speeches were long and confusing, but he was a persuasive **orator** nonetheless. King Louis XVI was beheaded in early 1793. Later that year, Robespierre won an appointment to the Committee of Public Safety, his first official position. The period from that appointment until Robespierre's death was known as the Reign of Terror.

Until his appointment on the Committee, Robespierre dealt with his opposition peacefully. With the power that came with his new position, he found that the guillotine was a fast, permanent solution to the problem of his **detractors.** He came to regard any challenge to his authority as an **affront** to France, which he served with such **magnanimity.** He perceived personal attacks on him as attacks on France. The ego he showed years earlier now demanded the executions of his enemies.

Earlier in his career he considered himself to be the protector of the downtrodden. After being appointed to the Committee, he began to consider himself to be the protector of the nation. The notion of the death penalty had once made him physically sick. He came to use it with shocking frequency, sending thousands—all "enemies of France"—to their deaths in less than a year. He believed he knew absolutely what his country needed, and he was not **encumbered** by doubt, pity, or remorse. At what seemed to be the height of his power, in the summer of 1794, his surviving enemies found the strength to arrest him and condemn him, along with a handful of supporters, to the guillotine. The Reign of Terror died with him.

Robespierre **cleaved** tightly to the belief that his actions were what his country demanded. His **dogma** and his methods made him the **despotic** forerunner to such nationalistic twentieth-century dictators as Hitler, Mussolini, and Stalin. He is remembered as the architect of the Reign of Terror. If he had possessed a little humility, he might be remembered as the father of modern France.

1. In this passage, **embody** means

   (A) represent.

   (B) champion.

   (C) celebrate.

   (D) endorse.

2. In the first paragraph, **incapacitated** means

   (A) made angry.

   (B) made sick.

   (C) made strong.

   (D) made helpless.

3. When did Robespierre's **contemporaries** live?

   (A) before he did

   (B) at the same time he did

   (C) after he did

   (D) in a different time than he did

4. An **orator**

   (A) listens.

   (B) gestures.

   (C) speaks.

   (D) writes.

5. An ANTONYM for **detractors** is

   (A) supporters.

   (B) enemies.

   (C) opponents.

   (D) hecklers.

6. A SYNONYM for **magnanimity** is

Ⓐ deceitfulness.

Ⓑ meanness.

Ⓒ selfishness.

Ⓓ selflessness.

7. In the seventh paragraph, "**cleaved** tightly to" means

Ⓐ ignored.

Ⓑ abandoned.

Ⓒ stood by.

Ⓓ endorsed.

8. Robespierre's **dogma** was something he

Ⓐ believed to be true.

Ⓑ believed to be desirable.

Ⓒ believed to be worthwhile.

Ⓓ believed to be wrong.

9. What is a **despotic** leader like?

Ⓐ kind

Ⓑ tyrannical

Ⓒ generous

Ⓓ enlightened

10. An ANTONYM for **impoverished** is

Ⓐ modest.

Ⓑ influential.

Ⓒ needy.

Ⓓ wealthy.

## Standardized Test Preview/Practice

1. **Impoverished** people are

   Ⓐ poor.

   Ⓑ oppressed.

   Ⓒ in trouble.

   Ⓓ outcasts.

   Ⓔ lucky.

2. In the first paragraph, **traumatic** most nearly means

   Ⓐ enjoyable.

   Ⓑ interesting.

   Ⓒ rewarding.

   Ⓓ emotional.

   Ⓔ empowering.

3. What best captures the meaning of the word **disseminate** in the second paragraph?

   Ⓐ announce

   Ⓑ spread

   Ⓒ publicize

   Ⓓ cover

   Ⓔ embellish

4. In the fifth paragraph, **affront** most nearly means

   Ⓐ insult.

   Ⓑ threat.

   Ⓒ compliment.

   Ⓓ attack.

   Ⓔ joke.

5. In the sixth paragraph, **encumbered** most nearly means

   Ⓐ delayed.

   Ⓑ endowed.

   Ⓒ concerned.

   Ⓓ troubled.

   Ⓔ burdened.

**Midterm Test 2**

Read the passage. Choose the best answer for each sentence or question about a bold word. Then fill in the circle next to your answer.

# The Last of the Seven Wonders

Of the Seven Wonders of the Ancient World, only Egypt's Great Pyramid at Giza still stands. It is the tomb of the pharaoh Khufu, and it was an **antiquity** even in **antiquity.** Its earliest history comes from a Greek traveler named Herodotus who visited Egypt nearly 2,500 years ago, when the pyramid was already 2,000 years old. With its **facets** covered in polished white limestone, it shone like a diamond rising from the desert. Light bounced off its surface like a mirror, and it could be seen from hundreds of miles away, even at night. Although the reflective surface was stolen ages ago, the monument is still an impressive sight.

The pyramid is made up of 2,300,000 blocks of stone. Each weighs about 2 1/2 tons. The sides are more than 750 feet long. All are within a few inches of the same length. The four sides face the four points of a compass—north, south, east, and west—perfectly. It is forty-five centuries old, and it remained the tallest structure on Earth for the first forty-three. Scholars have spent generations **speculating** about how the huge stone blocks of the pyramid were put into place so precisely with the **rudimentary** tools they had. Levers, ramps, sleds, and even space aliens have been considered as possible methods for moving the stone. The theory that the blocks were pushed or pulled up spiral ramps made slick with mud is accepted as the most **practicable** of the theories considered. Another puzzle to scientists is the question of how the pyramid was built so evenly, with evenly sloped and centered triangular sides. Some suggest that they measured the distance from a **plumb** line. Others believe the same ramp used to move the stones provided a level gauge of the pyramid's progress.

Despite the widely held belief that ancient enslaved people built the massive structure, experts believe that free Egyptians were more likely the workforce for the project. Every year when the river Nile flooded their farmland, farmers would come to Giza to work until the water receded. Some think they did it for the glory of Egypt and to **venerate** their king, but others think they may not have participated entirely of their own free will. They were most likely **remunerated** generously with food rather than with wages.

In ancient Egypt, all dead rulers were entombed with the **paraphernalia** of wealth, power, and comfort they might need in the next world. Many were buried with untold treasures, like the famous treasure of Tutankhamen, better known today as King Tut. The problem of how to protect the **consecrated** monuments from thieves is as old as the pyramids themselves. No matter how **ingenious** the pyramid designers were, they could not build a tomb that was truly **impervious** to robbers. Thieves in the 9th century decided to search for Khufu's fortune, and they found no trace of the pharaoh. Nobody knows what happened to Khufu's mummy and treasure. Some believe the treasure was stolen before that attempt. Some think the pyramid never held the riches at all. Still others think that the ancient wonder did its job perfectly, and continues to protect Khufu in his final place of **repose.**

1. In this passage, "in **antiquity**" means

    Ⓐ in Egypt.

    Ⓑ in the desert.

    Ⓒ in ancient times.

    Ⓓ in stories.

2. An ANTONYM for **rudimentary** is

    Ⓐ primitive.

    Ⓑ simple.

    Ⓒ expensive.

    Ⓓ advanced.

3. In the second paragraph, **practicable** means

    Ⓐ feasible.

    Ⓑ unlikely.

    Ⓒ complicated.

    Ⓓ popular.

4. A **plumb** line is

    Ⓐ level.

    Ⓑ crooked.

    Ⓒ dotted.

    Ⓓ vertical.

5. To **venerate** means

    Ⓐ to flatter.

    Ⓑ to show respect.

    Ⓒ to embarrass.

    Ⓓ to threaten.

6. A SYNONYM for **paraphernalia** is

    Ⓐ personal belongings.

    Ⓑ tributes.

    Ⓒ gifts.

    Ⓓ decoys.

7. In the fourth paragraph, **consecrated** means

　Ⓐ valuable.

　Ⓑ enormous.

　Ⓒ holy.

　Ⓓ tempting.

8. What is an **ingenious** designer like?

　Ⓐ determined

　Ⓑ happy

　Ⓒ lazy

　Ⓓ clever

9. To **repose** means to

　Ⓐ rest.

　Ⓑ celebrate.

　Ⓒ withdraw.

　Ⓓ escape.

10. In this passage, **remunerated** means

　Ⓐ charged.

　Ⓑ paid.

　Ⓒ fed.

　Ⓓ honored.

## Standardized Test Preview/Practice

1. To say the Great Pyramid was an **antiquity** means it was

   Ⓐ run down.

   Ⓑ valuable.

   Ⓒ from an ancient time.

   Ⓓ a popular attraction.

   Ⓔ unusual.

2. In the first paragraph, **facets** most nearly means

   Ⓐ stones.

   Ⓑ sides.

   Ⓒ windows.

   Ⓓ jewels.

   Ⓔ edges.

3. What best captures the meaning of the word **speculating** in the second paragraph?

   Ⓐ studying

   Ⓑ arguing

   Ⓒ researching

   Ⓓ testing

   Ⓔ guessing

4. In the third paragraph, **remunerated** most nearly means

   Ⓐ lured.

   Ⓑ rewarded.

   Ⓒ punished.

   Ⓓ bribed.

   Ⓔ motivated.

5. In the fourth paragraph, **impervious** most nearly means

   Ⓐ incapable of being penetrated.

   Ⓑ impossible to escape from.

   Ⓒ unconcerned about.

   Ⓓ frustrating.

   Ⓔ inviting.

**Lesson 11 Test**

**Find a SYNONYM for each bold word. Then fill in the circle next to your answer.**

1. Terri has an **aversion** to cold-blooded animals.

   Ⓐ fondness
   Ⓑ warmness
   Ⓒ opposition
   Ⓓ attraction

2. Chalmers works two jobs to **defray** the cost of his education and avoid borrowing.

   Ⓐ pay
   Ⓑ defer
   Ⓒ extend
   Ⓓ forgive

3. Personal computers have **superseded** typewriters as the most popular tool for word processing.

   Ⓐ dominated
   Ⓑ subjugated
   Ⓒ joined
   Ⓓ replaced

4. The administration was caught off guard by the **furor** over the decision to stop offering the salad bar in the cafeteria.

   Ⓐ uproar
   Ⓑ silence
   Ⓒ calm
   Ⓓ serenity

5. The manager wrote the weekly schedule on a calendar so it would be **tangible** for all involved.

   Ⓐ vague
   Ⓑ understandable
   Ⓒ indistinct
   Ⓓ uncertain

**Find an ANTONYM for each bold word. Then fill in the circle next to your answer.**

6. Waiting until the last minute to register meant Terry had to choose from the **paucity** of elective options that were still available.

   Ⓐ abundance
   Ⓑ scarcity
   Ⓒ insufficiency
   Ⓓ lack

7. Dad tried to provide one last **idyllic** summer weekend before school started again.

   Ⓐ calm
   Ⓑ pleasant
   Ⓒ carefree
   Ⓓ traumatic

8. Among the **amenities** in the community were all the shops within walking distance.

  Ⓐ comforts

  Ⓑ detriments

  Ⓒ bonuses

  Ⓓ conveniences

9. **Complacency** is the enemy of improvement.

  Ⓐ concern

  Ⓑ satisfaction

  Ⓒ contentment

  Ⓓ calm

10. The formula failed because it was based on a **fallacious** assumption.

  Ⓐ wrong

  Ⓑ mistaken

  Ⓒ correct

  Ⓓ untrue

**Choose the best way to complete each sentence or answer each question. Then fill in the circle next to your answer.**

11. What remains after an animal has **decomposed?**

  Ⓐ roots

  Ⓑ sprouts

  Ⓒ skin

  Ⓓ elements

12. Which of the following does not describe a **facetious** remark's tone?

  Ⓐ serious

  Ⓑ joking

  Ⓒ playful

  Ⓓ kidding

13. In paying attention to **amenities,** one would not display

  Ⓐ manners.

  Ⓑ courtesy.

  Ⓒ aggression.

  Ⓓ politeness.

14. Where are things **envisaged?**

  Ⓐ in books

  Ⓑ in the mind

  Ⓒ in photographs

  Ⓓ in museums

15. Which of the following is the least **porous?**

  Ⓐ sponge

  Ⓑ marble

  Ⓒ Swiss cheese

  Ⓓ cotton ball

## Standardized Test Preview/Practice

In this passage, some of the words from this lesson are in bold. Read the passage and then answer the questions.

The **paucity** of inexpensive options for vacations that please the whole family can make parents of teens very stressed. Sharing hotel rooms isn't easy with grown children, but getting extra rooms is often too expensive.

5 Going camping is a popular choice for many families trying to work within a budget, but this option can cause conflict. Teens may think **amenities** such as Internet access and cell-phone service are absolutely essential. Many are **averse** to going without daily showers and hate the idea

10 of using a chemical toilet instead of one that flushes. What seems **idyllic** to parents seeking time in nature can feel like a nightmare to their children. The parents may love the smell of **decomposing** leaves or enjoy the sound of rain as it hits their tent, but their teens may be holding their noses and

15 complaining loudly about being unable to sleep.

1. In line 1, **paucity** means

   Ⓐ variety.

   Ⓑ lack.

   Ⓒ choice.

   Ⓓ number.

2. The word **amenities** (line 7) most nearly means

   Ⓐ technicalities.

   Ⓑ social courtesies.

   Ⓒ things that are nice to have.

   Ⓓ necessary items.

3. The phrase "are **averse** to" (line 9) most nearly means

   Ⓐ like.

   Ⓑ are opposed to.

   Ⓒ are pleased by.

   Ⓓ look forward to.

4. In line 11, **idyllic** means

   Ⓐ peaceful and relaxing.

   Ⓑ tolerable.

   Ⓒ exciting.

   Ⓓ important.

5. The word **decomposing** (line 13) most nearly means

   Ⓐ wet.

   Ⓑ fall.

   Ⓒ decaying.

   Ⓓ fresh.

Name _____  Date _____

**Find a SYNONYM for each bold word. Then fill in the circle next to your answer.**

1. Marla found it hard to **empathize** with people whose experiences were so different from her own.

Ⓐ console
Ⓑ understand
Ⓒ pity
Ⓓ criticize

2. Since Molly was soaking wet when she arrived, Aidan **inferred** that it was raining outside.

Ⓐ deduced
Ⓑ doubted
Ⓒ considered
Ⓓ saw

3. Diabetes often **manifests** itself as a persistent thirst.

Ⓐ masks
Ⓑ hides
Ⓒ disguises
Ⓓ reveals

4. George's skilled artist's eye could see the **nuances** that separated sage green from moss green.

Ⓐ borders
Ⓑ gradations
Ⓒ similarities
Ⓓ colors

5. Though she knew it would never be published, Cynthia spent years working on her **treatise** on junk food through the ages.

Ⓐ composition
Ⓑ collage
Ⓒ play
Ⓓ speech

**Find an ANTONYM for each bold word. Then fill in the circle next to your answer.**

6. Cody kept a positive attitude even when faced with **adversity.**

Ⓐ hardship
Ⓑ misfortune
Ⓒ advantage
Ⓓ disability

7. Simon had a few **cardinal** rules for borrowing his books.

Ⓐ important
Ⓑ chief
Ⓒ major
Ⓓ minor

8. Max's explanation for why the chair was on the roof was not **credible.**

   Ⓐ suspicious

   Ⓑ believable

   Ⓒ true

   Ⓓ reliable

9. Although Sabra had never been to New York before, she had an **intuitive** feeling that this city would be a great fit for her.

   Ⓐ outrageous

   Ⓑ spontaneous

   Ⓒ fearful

   Ⓓ reasoned

10. Josh found the competition so **harrowing** that even though he won, he vowed never to do it again.

   Ⓐ distressing

   Ⓑ painful

   Ⓒ enjoyable

   Ⓓ unusual

**Choose the best way to complete each sentence or answer each question. Then fill in the circle next to your answer.**

11. Which of the following would not be one of a person's **faculties?**

   Ⓐ thinking

   Ⓑ juggling

   Ⓒ hearing

   Ⓓ seeing

12. You might draw an **inference** based on what?

   Ⓐ evidence

   Ⓑ arguments

   Ⓒ luck

   Ⓓ disability

13. "Blue jeans never seem to go out of **vogue**" means that they are always

   Ⓐ in fashion.

   Ⓑ in demand.

   Ⓒ classic.

   Ⓓ casual.

14. Which of these is most likely to be an **impairment** to a quick vacation abroad?

   Ⓐ fear of flying

   Ⓑ hotel reservations

   Ⓒ passport

   Ⓓ luggage

15. Who is least likely to need **solace?**

   Ⓐ a grieving widow

   Ⓑ a robbery victim

   Ⓒ a jackpot winner

   Ⓓ the loser of a tennis match

## Standardized Test Preview/Practice

**In this passage, some of the words from this lesson are in bold. Read the passage and then answer the questions.**

With today's technology, it is possible to earn a college degree without ever stepping onto a college campus or attending class in person. Online learning is a good option, but those considering this idea should be careful.

5   While many well-respected colleges and universities have online courses that are taught by excellent **faculty,** the for-profit online-education industry doesn't have the same kind of **credibility.** It has been discovered that several have included **pernicious** lies in their advertising about job-placement rates

10   to attract more students.

A student who has chosen to attend such an online college, and who then graduates expecting to find a job easily, may instead go through the **harrowing** experience of not being able to find a job to pay off his or her college loans.

15   Students are wise to be cautious and trust their **intuition** if they sense something isn't right about an online college and its promises.

1. In line 6, **faculty** means
   Ⓐ natural powers.
   Ⓑ professors.
   Ⓒ abilities.
   Ⓓ classrooms.

2. In line 8, the word **credibility** most nearly means
   Ⓐ trustworthy reputation.
   Ⓑ teaching staff.
   Ⓒ technical access.
   Ⓓ image.

3. The meaning of **pernicious** (line 9) is
   Ⓐ secret.
   Ⓑ false.
   Ⓒ harmful.
   Ⓓ unwise.

4. The word **harrowing** (line 13) most nearly means
   Ⓐ extremely upsetting.
   Ⓑ slightly unpleasant.
   Ⓒ satisfying.
   Ⓓ interesting.

5. The meaning of **intuition** (line 15) is
   Ⓐ judgment.
   Ⓑ innate feelings.
   Ⓒ decision.
   Ⓓ information.

Name _____   Date _____

**Find a SYNONYM for each bold word. Then fill in the circle next to your answer.**

1. The song's rise to the top of the chart had been **meteoric.**

   Ⓐ slow
   Ⓑ indirect
   Ⓒ fast
   Ⓓ surprising

2. Taylor's **precocity** in music had emerged by his third birthday.

   Ⓐ aptitude
   Ⓑ intuition
   Ⓒ reputation
   Ⓓ enjoyment

3. The science club was thrilled by the lab's **proffer** of meeting space and experimental materials.

   Ⓐ suggestion
   Ⓑ offer
   Ⓒ request
   Ⓓ mention

4. To distinguish himself from his voluble twin, Brett tried to be more **succinct.**

   Ⓐ quiet
   Ⓑ wordy
   Ⓒ concise
   Ⓓ kind

5. Jesse faced the principal with **trepidation.**

   Ⓐ dread
   Ⓑ confidence
   Ⓒ relaxation
   Ⓓ anger

**Find an ANTONYM for each bold word. Then fill in the circle next to your answer.**

6. Jack grew weary of Bobby's always **deprecating** any new idea.

   Ⓐ criticizing
   Ⓑ belittling
   Ⓒ embracing
   Ⓓ ignoring

7. Try not to **discomfit** newcomers with too many personal questions.

   Ⓐ calm
   Ⓑ embarrass
   Ⓒ taunt
   Ⓓ perplex

8. Maria was careful not to trip on the **rift** in the sidewalk.

Ⓐ crack

Ⓑ break

Ⓒ turn

Ⓓ repair

9. Isabella's **overbearing** manner annoyed her coworkers.

Ⓐ pushy

Ⓑ submissive

Ⓒ domineering

Ⓓ arrogant

10. Getting a flat tire on the way to a job interview is particularly **untoward.**

Ⓐ favorable

Ⓑ unlucky

Ⓒ frustrating

Ⓓ ominous

**Choose the best way to complete each sentence or answer each question. Then fill in the circle next to your answer.**

11. A child is most likely to **remonstrate** with a parent about which of the following?

Ⓐ bedtime

Ⓑ playtime

Ⓒ lunchtime

Ⓓ anytime

12. A **virtuoso** performance is most likely to be

Ⓐ funny.

Ⓑ boring.

Ⓒ long.

Ⓓ excellent.

13. **Blandishments** are not intended to

Ⓐ coax.

Ⓑ persuade.

Ⓒ threaten.

Ⓓ convince.

14. A **sylvan** setting is full of

Ⓐ animals.

Ⓑ buildings.

Ⓒ lakes.

Ⓓ trees.

15. Which of the following is a **solicitous** friend least likely to do?

Ⓐ forget your birthday

Ⓑ help you move

Ⓒ visit you in the hospital

Ⓓ cheer you up

## Standardized Test Preview/Practice

**In this passage, some of the words from this lesson are in bold. Read the passage and then answer the questions.**

When I arrived at the dance studio, Denali was staring at herself in the mirror, her arms crossed, frowning at her reflection. She was dressed in a bright skirt and a black leotard, ready for her performance at the African Festival.

5    "I keep messing up. I guess I just wasn't born with rhythm," she said sourly. Nothing could have been further from the truth, but she tended to **deprecate** herself when she was nervous.

"Are you kidding me? You were born with rhythm, energy,
10    grace… uh…" I paused, trying to think of more ways to bolster her confidence. She turned and put up her hand to silence me before I could **proffer** any more **blandishments.**

"You're just biased because you're my friend!"

"Listen," I said firmly. "I know you feel some **trepidation.**
15    That's natural. But you're going to be great tonight. You practiced all week."

Denali turned back to the mirror. She tilted her head at her reflection, sighed, and placed both hands on her hips, rocking back and forth on her heels.

20    I patted her shoulder in my usual **solicitous** way. "You are going to be great," I repeated. "Trust me."

1. In line 7, **deprecate** most nearly means
   Ⓐ look at.
   Ⓑ isolate.
   Ⓒ criticize.
   Ⓓ represent.

2. The meaning of **proffer** (line 12) is
   Ⓐ offer.
   Ⓑ yell.
   Ⓒ sell.
   Ⓓ take.

3. In line 12, **blandishments** means
   Ⓐ insults.
   Ⓑ flattering words.
   Ⓒ pieces of advice.
   Ⓓ unnecessary information.

4. The word **trepidation** (line 14) most nearly means
   Ⓐ excitement.
   Ⓑ hope.
   Ⓒ fear.
   Ⓓ despair.

5. In line 20, **solicitous** means
   Ⓐ unfriendly.
   Ⓑ concerned.
   Ⓒ soft.
   Ⓓ playful.

Name _____     Date _____

**Find a SYNONYM for each bold word. Then fill in the circle next to your answer.**

1. The toddler's vocabulary grew faster than his ability to **articulate** the words he was learning.

   Ⓐ pronounce
   Ⓑ understand
   Ⓒ apply
   Ⓓ recognize

2. Billy was determined to **decimate** the aphids before they ate his rosebushes.

   Ⓐ nourish
   Ⓑ kill
   Ⓒ repel
   Ⓓ embrace

3. Risk is an **inherent** part of investing.

   Ⓐ unfortunate
   Ⓑ undesirable
   Ⓒ avoidable
   Ⓓ built-in

4. The class was embarrassed when Ms. Wright caught them **parodying** her accent.

   Ⓐ imitating
   Ⓑ discussing
   Ⓒ filming
   Ⓓ noticing

5. It was hard for someone as **gregarious** as Laura to be alone for very long.

   Ⓐ popular
   Ⓑ bored
   Ⓒ sociable
   Ⓓ eager

**Find an ANTONYM for each bold word. Then fill in the circle next to your answer.**

6. Carla spent a month **amassing** thousands of signatures on the petition.

   Ⓐ gathering
   Ⓑ dispersing
   Ⓒ collecting
   Ⓓ accumulating

7. Roxana had never displayed such **pugnacity** before in her life.

   Ⓐ passiveness
   Ⓑ aggression
   Ⓒ belligerence
   Ⓓ rudeness

8. Jude bewailed his **reprehensible** involvement in the caper.

   Ⓐ regretful

   Ⓑ innocent

   Ⓒ accidental

   Ⓓ deliberate

9. Thanks to Luke's calling 911 immediately, the fire was still **tractable** when help arrived.

   Ⓐ burning

   Ⓑ destructive

   Ⓒ contained

   Ⓓ unmanageable

10. Rather than giving a straightforward book report, Clyde chose to surprise his teacher with a **zany** skit depicting his favorite scene.

    Ⓐ clownish

    Ⓑ comical

    Ⓒ serious

    Ⓓ funny

**Choose the best way to complete each sentence or answer each question. Then fill in the circle next to your answer.**

11. With which of the following are you least likely to **garb** yourself?

    Ⓐ bathrobe

    Ⓑ shampoo

    Ⓒ pajamas

    Ⓓ shower cap

12. Another word for **maternal** is

    Ⓐ fatherly.

    Ⓑ brotherly.

    Ⓒ sisterly.

    Ⓓ motherly.

13. If good manners are the result of **nurture,** they come from one's

    Ⓐ inherited aptitudes.

    Ⓑ luck.

    Ⓒ dedicated studying.

    Ⓓ upbringing.

14. Which of the following is least **obtrusive?**

    Ⓐ a bull in a china shop

    Ⓑ a hose in a garden

    Ⓒ a dog in a courtroom

    Ⓓ a cat in a cradle

15. What does one use to **articulate** something?

    Ⓐ pictures

    Ⓑ words

    Ⓒ gestures

    Ⓓ ideas

## Standardized Test Preview/Practice

**In this passage, some of the words from this lesson are in bold. Read the passage and then answer the questions.**

Hiro wanted to join the Drama Club. He wasn't the most **gregarious** person, but he liked the idea of socializing with people who loved acting, comedy, and theater as much as he did. So, despite the fact that he wasn't very outgoing, he
5 signed up.

The first meeting was much more fun than he could have ever imagined. He and the other members played some warm-up games, in which each person **articulated** his or her reasons for joining. One new girl said she wanted to star in a
10 Broadway musical someday. No one laughed; instead, they all encouraged her to sing a song, and she did. She was amazing!

That made Hiro brave enough to tell everyone he acted out **parodies** of his favorite reality TV shows and uploaded them to the Internet. Before he knew it, he was acting out
15 his favorite TV chef's **dexterous** and theatrical handling of pots and pans, mimicking his **obtrusive** personality, yelling at people and lunging around an imaginary kitchen. By the time the meeting ended, Hiro had made two new friends, and lots of people had told him they'd subscribe to his video channel.
20 He was so glad he'd joined the club!

1. The word **gregarious** (line 2) most nearly means
   Ⓐ quiet.
   Ⓑ confident.
   Ⓒ sociable.
   Ⓓ talented.

2. In line 8, **articulated** means
   Ⓐ explained.
   Ⓑ whispered.
   Ⓒ acted out.
   Ⓓ wrote.

3. The meaning of **parodies** (line 13) is
   Ⓐ dramas.
   Ⓑ reviews.
   Ⓒ imitations.
   Ⓓ jokes.

4. In line 15, **dexterous** means
   Ⓐ fancy.
   Ⓑ skillful.
   Ⓒ forceful.
   Ⓓ careful.

5. The meaning of **obtrusive** (line 16) is
   Ⓐ mean.
   Ⓑ comical.
   Ⓒ pushy.
   Ⓓ interesting.

**Lesson**
**15** **Test**

**Find a SYNONYM for each bold word. Then fill in the circle next to your answer.**

1. Many long hours practicing were **antecedent** to Kerri's triumph at the tournament.

   Ⓐ unrelated
   Ⓑ preceding
   Ⓒ coincidental
   Ⓓ subsequent

2. Breaking her previous record by several seconds was **indubitable** proof that the sprinter had been training seriously.

   Ⓐ unquestionable
   Ⓑ likely
   Ⓒ probable
   Ⓓ suspicious

3. We gathered enough **momentum** on the downhill part of the trail to carry us up the hill at the end.

   Ⓐ energy
   Ⓑ determination
   Ⓒ breath
   Ⓓ support

4. Dark clouds represented a **potential** flaw in the plan for a perfect day outdoors.

   Ⓐ growing
   Ⓑ unexpected
   Ⓒ unlikely
   Ⓓ possible

5. Her mother insisted that Rachel begin to exercise her **volition** in everyday matters.

   Ⓐ power
   Ⓑ choice
   Ⓒ reason
   Ⓓ responsibility

**Find an ANTONYM for each bold word. Then fill in the circle next to your answer.**

6. The divide between industrialized and developing nations is **accentuated** by the infant mortality rate.

   Ⓐ emphasized
   Ⓑ minimized
   Ⓒ intensified
   Ⓓ stressed

7. A classical music **aficionado,** Derrick had season tickets to the symphony.

   Ⓐ detractor
   Ⓑ fan
   Ⓒ supporter
   Ⓓ follower

8. Sam had a **visceral** reaction to the Holocaust documentary.

Ⓐ powerful

Ⓑ strong

Ⓒ mild

Ⓓ allergic

9. Melissa was frustrated by the **disingenuous** way Liz cancelled their plans.

Ⓐ awkward

Ⓑ insincere

Ⓒ indirect

Ⓓ straightforward

10. The family became **jaded** about eating lobster after a year in Maine.

Ⓐ weary

Ⓑ excited

Ⓒ dulled

Ⓓ distrustful

**Choose the best way to complete each sentence or answer each question. Then fill in the circle next to your answer.**

11. **Centrifugal** has to do with something's relative position to the

Ⓐ edge.

Ⓑ corner.

Ⓒ center.

Ⓓ surface.

12. Origami is the Japanese art of making **convoluted** shapes from single sheets of paper. It involves

Ⓐ cutting.

Ⓑ folding.

Ⓒ gluing.

Ⓓ coloring.

13. What body part is involved in **decapitating?**

Ⓐ the head

Ⓑ the arms

Ⓒ the hands

Ⓓ the legs

14. A **masochistic** person is one who enjoys

Ⓐ books.

Ⓑ sleep.

Ⓒ exercise.

Ⓓ pain.

15. If something is **obsolescent,** how likely are you to see it in use?

Ⓐ very

Ⓑ somewhat

Ⓒ moderately

Ⓓ hardly at all

## Standardized Test Preview/Practice

**In this passage, some of the words from this lesson are in bold. Read the passage and then answer the questions.**

"Fans of horror movies must be **masochists!** After all, it can't be fun to watch blood and gore and **viscera** just splash across the screen! That stuff makes me cringe!" Jorge said, shivering. It was getting close to Halloween, and we were
5  sitting in our seats at the movie theater. We'd just watched two trailers for horror movies. They were pretty tame, actually, and a little funny to me. Same old scary music, same old tricks to make viewers jump out of their seats.

"I must be **jaded,** because horror movies make me laugh,"
10  I said, grabbing a handful of popcorn from the bucket we were sharing. "I wouldn't go to one of my own **volition,**" I admitted, "but the gory scenes are so fake, they're funny."

"Come on," Jorge said, "don't be **disingenuous.** You must get a little scared, or at least disgusted!"

15  "I'm being totally honest," I said. "If you make it through two or three horror movies, you'll see how they're all alike and how hard the filmmakers are trying to scare you. Then you'll just laugh because they're ridiculous and predictable."

1. In line 1, **masochists** means

   Ⓐ people who are crazy.

   Ⓑ people who are stupid.

   Ⓒ people who enjoy pain.

   Ⓓ people who like movies.

2. The word **viscera** (line 2) most nearly means

   Ⓐ special effects.

   Ⓑ internal organs of the body.

   Ⓒ liquids.

   Ⓓ dead bodies.

3. In line 9, **jaded** most nearly means

   Ⓐ too bored.

   Ⓑ frightened.

   Ⓒ too used to it to be affected.

   Ⓓ worried.

4. The phrase "of my own **volition**" (line 11) most nearly means

   Ⓐ voluntarily.

   Ⓑ without adult supervision.

   Ⓒ by myself.

   Ⓓ with enthusiasm.

5. In line 13, **disingenuous** means

   Ⓐ obnoxious.

   Ⓑ silly.

   Ⓒ unkind.

   Ⓓ insincere.

Name _____    Date _____

## Test

**Find a SYNONYM for each bold word. Then fill in the circle next to your answer.**

1. Dennis boldly **contravened** the school's directive about leaving the grounds during the day.

   Ⓐ obeyed
   Ⓑ defied
   Ⓒ supported
   Ⓓ enforced

2. The **default** delivery method is surface mail; please check the "air mail" box if you wish for a faster delivery.

   Ⓐ automatic
   Ⓑ preferred
   Ⓒ cheapest
   Ⓓ popular

3. Banners **emblazoned** with team colors were hung all around the stadium.

   Ⓐ written
   Ⓑ pictured
   Ⓒ decorated
   Ⓓ described

4. Steven was nervous about his performance because he was just a **novice** at lacrosse.

   Ⓐ substitute
   Ⓑ regular
   Ⓒ expert
   Ⓓ beginner

5. Despite her age, Aunt Myrtle was **spry** on the dance floor.

   Ⓐ stiff
   Ⓑ clumsy
   Ⓒ lively
   Ⓓ awkward

**Find an ANTONYM for each bold word. Then fill in the circle next to your answer.**

6. To his **chagrin,** Dante tripped while trying to sneak up on Beatrice.

   Ⓐ embarrassment
   Ⓑ delight
   Ⓒ annoyance
   Ⓓ unease

7. Marc's **doldrums** continued for weeks after moving to a new city.

   Ⓐ moodiness
   Ⓑ indifference
   Ⓒ contentment
   Ⓓ melancholy

8. A Pulitzer Prize is proof of a writer's **eminence.**

Ⓐ power

Ⓑ averageness

Ⓒ prestige

Ⓓ talent

9. Richard **expended** so much energy preparing for the game that he was too tired to enjoy it.

Ⓐ stored

Ⓑ wasted

Ⓒ used

Ⓓ spent

10. The coat was held together by a few **tenuous** threads.

Ⓐ thin

Ⓑ flimsy

Ⓒ weak

Ⓓ thick

**Choose the best way to complete each sentence or answer each question. Then fill in the circle next to your answer.**

11. A **belated** action is performed

Ⓐ early.

Ⓑ on time.

Ⓒ late.

Ⓓ not at all.

12. How might someone **default** on a loan?

Ⓐ by paying the loan on time

Ⓑ by missing a loan payment

Ⓒ by taking out a loan

Ⓓ by paying off a loan completely

13. When a password **expires,** it

Ⓐ no longer works.

Ⓑ becomes public.

Ⓒ gets renewed.

Ⓓ must be reset.

14. Which of the following is the most **tenuous?**

Ⓐ helium

Ⓑ iron

Ⓒ cardboard

Ⓓ cotton

15. How well known is a **truism** likely to be?

Ⓐ not at all

Ⓑ a little bit

Ⓒ somewhat

Ⓓ very

## Standardized Test Preview/Practice

In this passage, some of the words from this lesson are in bold. Read the passage and then answer the questions.

To her **chagrin,** Pilar learned that the **eminent** biologist she'd idolized since she was a child wasn't going to come speak at her school after all. Pilar and her classmates in Honors Biology had been looking forward to the visit for six months,
5 when it was suddenly canceled. It wasn't often that an award-winning scientist of such high **caliber** made it all the way out to the rural area where she lived. In fact, Pilar had never met a working biologist at all and really wanted to ask her some questions.
10 Pilar's biology teacher, Ms. Assad, had arranged the visit through a **tenuous** connection—Ms. Assad's second cousin had worked in the same research laboratory. Pilar was disappointed but didn't lose hope. Her teacher was a big **exponent** of connecting young women to leaders in the
15 science, math, and technology fields. She knew Ms. Assad would find another biologist willing to trek out to the middle of nowhere to talk to her class. It was just a matter of time.

1. The phrase "to her **chagrin**" (line 1) most nearly means

   Ⓐ to her disappointment.
   Ⓑ with shame.
   Ⓒ not surprisingly.
   Ⓓ to her delight.

2. In line 1, **eminent** means

   Ⓐ intelligent.
   Ⓑ well-known.
   Ⓒ female.
   Ⓓ academic.

3. The word **caliber** (line 6) most nearly means

   Ⓐ diameter.
   Ⓑ cost.
   Ⓒ social status.
   Ⓓ rank.

4. In line 11, **tenuous** most nearly means

   Ⓐ unimportant.
   Ⓑ work-related.
   Ⓒ not very strong.
   Ⓓ family-related.

5. In line 14, the phrase "**exponent** of" most nearly means

   Ⓐ proponent of.
   Ⓑ enemy of.
   Ⓒ explainer of.
   Ⓓ examiner of.

Name _____ Date _____

**Find a SYNONYM for each bold word. Then fill in the circle next to your answer.**

1. Ms. Diaz's library was **cited** for constantly innovating.

   Ⓐ noted
   Ⓑ punished
   Ⓒ rebuked
   Ⓓ praised

2. While she did not claim to be innocent, the prisoner appealed to the governor for **clemency.**

   Ⓐ release
   Ⓑ mercy
   Ⓒ favors
   Ⓓ sentencing

3. From a shoebox of letters, photos, and keepsakes, I **gleaned** that my grandparents had once been young and crazy about each other.

   Ⓐ guessed
   Ⓑ understood
   Ⓒ gathered
   Ⓓ disagreed

4. Lawrence was thrilled when the judge **quashed** the injunction prohibiting him from selling the historic home.

   Ⓐ stopped
   Ⓑ upheld
   Ⓒ reduced
   Ⓓ strengthened

5. Grandma's **verve** is apparent at her famous parties.

   Ⓐ dourness
   Ⓑ vivacity
   Ⓒ creepiness
   Ⓓ popularity

**Find an ANTONYM for each bold word. Then fill in the circle next to your answer.**

6. Smoking had **blighted** Leslie's beautiful smile.

   Ⓐ damaged
   Ⓑ benefited
   Ⓒ harmed
   Ⓓ ruined

7. The drama club produced a **farce** about electronic communication gone haywire.

   Ⓐ play
   Ⓑ comedy
   Ⓒ musical
   Ⓓ drama

8. Ms. McCalla remained the **nominal** editor-in-chief long after she stopped being involved in day-to-day operations at the magazine.

   Ⓐ actual

   Ⓑ dedicated

   Ⓒ devoted

   Ⓓ ceremonial

9. Chuck was afraid he would be **ostracized** from the group once the truth about his past emerged.

   Ⓐ banned

   Ⓑ removed

   Ⓒ included

   Ⓓ suspended

10. We were the **recipients** of Alfredo's hospitality when we traveled to Guatemala.

    Ⓐ donors

    Ⓑ targets

    Ⓒ receivers

    Ⓓ guests

**Choose the best way to complete each sentence or answer each question. Then fill in the circle next to your answer.**

11. When drivers are **cited** for traffic violations, where are they being summoned to appear?

    Ⓐ in a court of law

    Ⓑ in traffic school

    Ⓒ at the police station

    Ⓓ in a driver's education class

12. The behavior of an **eccentric** is all of the following except

    Ⓐ peculiar.

    Ⓑ ordinary.

    Ⓒ odd.

    Ⓓ unusual.

13. When is a **posthumous** award given?

    Ⓐ after retirement

    Ⓑ before dinner

    Ⓒ after death

    Ⓓ before promotion

14. Susan B. Anthony was a crusader for women's **suffrage.** What right did she want?

    Ⓐ to own property

    Ⓑ to bear arms

    Ⓒ to vote

    Ⓓ to assemble

15. If you participate in a **foray,** where will you find yourself?

    Ⓐ in enemy territory

    Ⓑ at a lively party

    Ⓒ at a neighbor's home

    Ⓓ in a peaceful sanctuary

## Standardized Test Preview/Practice

**In this passage, some of the words from this lesson are in bold. Read the passage and then answer the questions.**

There are many things that make an old-fashioned county fair unique. While many have the same rides as amusement parks do, they tend to charge less for entry and also have some charming traditions that make attending one a fun and
5    worthwhile experience.

One tradition is the contests. For example, farmers grow "monster" pumpkins and zucchini squash and then pay a **nominal** fee just to enter a contest to see who grew the biggest and best. Contest judges carefully check for **blight**
10   with magnifying glasses and measure and weigh each giant gourd as the eager crowd watches. Usually everyone agrees on the winner of these contests, but the pie and baking competitions are different. These can be seen as a **farce** because the same people often win year after year. Lastly,
15   many fairs feature a different kind of "contest": reenactments of historical military battles, in which people dressed as soldiers pretend to make **forays** into "enemy territory."

One of the oldest county fairs, held annually in Fryeburg, Maine, includes night performances by entertainers.
20   All performers make sure their shows are family-friendly. For example, comedians try not to tell **ribald** jokes or use language that would not be appropriate for children. Thus, this county fair—like all others—remains a great way for families to have fun together.

1. The word **nominal** (line 8) most nearly means

  Ⓐ in name only.

  Ⓑ small.

  Ⓒ outrageous.

  Ⓓ large.

2. The meaning of **blight** (line 9) is

  Ⓐ crime.

  Ⓑ disease.

  Ⓒ color.

  Ⓓ flaws.

3. The phrase "seen as a **farce**" (line 13) most nearly means

  Ⓐ viewed as comedy.

  Ⓑ seen as authentic.

  Ⓒ seen as inauthentic.

  Ⓓ viewed humorously.

4. In line 17, the phrase "make **forays** into" means

  Ⓐ invade.

  Ⓑ judge.

  Ⓒ look into.

  Ⓓ create.

5. The word **ribald** (line 21) most nearly means

  Ⓐ funny.

  Ⓑ bad.

  Ⓒ crude and inappropriate.

  Ⓓ advanced.

### Lesson 18 Test

**Find a SYNONYM for each bold word. Then fill in the circle next to your answer.**

1. The economic advisor was an **adherent** to the philosophy of *laissez-faire,* so he rarely recommended intervening.

   Ⓐ follower
   Ⓑ detractor
   Ⓒ skeptic
   Ⓓ expert

2. Though her knees were knocking, Paula conducted the interview of her idol with complete **aplomb.**

   Ⓐ terror
   Ⓑ poise
   Ⓒ awkwardness
   Ⓓ professionalism

3. Tom delicately **broached** the subject of a summer abroad.

   Ⓐ sidestepped
   Ⓑ raised
   Ⓒ pondered
   Ⓓ considered

4. With practice and patience, Earl **surmounted** his phobia of public speaking.

   Ⓐ overcame
   Ⓑ accepted
   Ⓒ exercised
   Ⓓ embraced

5. Lori was **resplendent** in her wedding gown.

   Ⓐ uncomfortable
   Ⓑ acceptable
   Ⓒ sweet
   Ⓓ dazzling

**Find an ANTONYM for each bold word. Then fill in the circle next to your answer.**

6. Military authority is built on **adherence** to the chain of command.

   Ⓐ departing
   Ⓑ orders
   Ⓒ sticking
   Ⓓ following

7. Julia is a **devotee** of yoga.

   Ⓐ enthusiast
   Ⓑ practitioner
   Ⓒ opponent
   Ⓓ proponent

8. No matter how many times she did it, Diane was always **diffident** walking into a new classroom.

Ⓐ shy

Ⓑ confident

Ⓒ unsure

Ⓓ uneasy

9. Spot's **plaintive** stare at the empty food bowl prevented Drew from enforcing the dog's diet.

Ⓐ sad

Ⓑ mournful

Ⓒ happy

Ⓓ pitiful

10. Our special graduation **regalia** consists of a cap and gown.

Ⓐ garb

Ⓑ rags

Ⓒ costume

Ⓓ outfit

**Choose the best way to complete each sentence or answer each question. Then fill in the circle next to your answer.**

11. To **brandish** something is an attempt to do all of the following except

Ⓐ threaten.

Ⓑ intimidate.

Ⓒ soothe.

Ⓓ menace.

12. There was an **extravaganza** when the local team won the national championship. The event was all of the following except

Ⓐ elaborate.

Ⓑ spectacular.

Ⓒ showy.

Ⓓ tame.

13. If the paper straw you are using loses its **integrity** before you finish your drink, what happens to the straw?

Ⓐ It changes color.

Ⓑ It falls apart.

Ⓒ It becomes stronger.

Ⓓ It gets lost.

14. To **subordinate** your own wants for a greater cause means to

Ⓐ make the cause more important than your wants.

Ⓑ make your wants more important than the cause.

Ⓒ work equally toward both goals.

Ⓓ choose one or the other.

15. If something is **tenable,** it is

Ⓐ reasonable.

Ⓑ outrageous.

Ⓒ impossible.

Ⓓ unattractive.

## Standardized Test Preview/Practice

**In this passage, some of the words from this lesson are in bold. Read the passage and then answer the questions.**

It's interesting how people behave when we meet celebrities. Regular people often act **diffident** around a celebrity, as if we were **subordinate** to the famous person. People have even been known to faint or cry after meeting a
5  celebrity they admire! The more **plaudits** and attention the celebrity gets, or the more **resplendent** he or she looks, the less comfortable some of us feel. Whether the celebrity is a kind or honest person with **integrity** doesn't seem to matter to us in the moment, as long as he or she is famous.
10  However, fame is often temporary, and celebrity has nothing to do with your talent or worth as a human being. Try to keep some perspective if you meet someone famous. Take a deep breath and remember that we're all just human!

1.  The meaning of **diffident** (line 2) is

    Ⓐ embarrassed.

    Ⓑ excited.

    Ⓒ unsure of themselves.

    Ⓓ terrified.

2.  The phrase "**subordinate** to" (line 3) most nearly means

    Ⓐ lesser than.

    Ⓑ closer to.

    Ⓒ better than.

    Ⓓ next to.

3.  The meaning of **plaudits** (line 5) is

    Ⓐ photos.

    Ⓑ interviews.

    Ⓒ praise.

    Ⓓ time.

4.  In line 6, **resplendent** means

    Ⓐ snobby.

    Ⓑ dazzling.

    Ⓒ famous.

    Ⓓ distracted.

5.  The word **integrity** (line 8) most nearly means

    Ⓐ honesty.

    Ⓑ wisdom.

    Ⓒ intellect.

    Ⓓ wholeness.

## Lesson 19 Test

**Find a SYNONYM for each bold word. Then fill in the circle next to your answer.**

1. Fear of heights prevented Ryan from reaching the **apex** of the Eiffel Tower.

   Ⓐ center
   Ⓑ base
   Ⓒ top
   Ⓓ vicinity

2. During India's struggle for independence, Gandhi went on several hunger strikes and was ready to be **martyred** for the cause.

   Ⓐ publicized
   Ⓑ ridiculed
   Ⓒ killed
   Ⓓ jailed

3. A **multitude** assembled to catch a glimpse of the candidate on her stop in town.

   Ⓐ lot
   Ⓑ crowd
   Ⓒ trio
   Ⓓ demonstration

4. Placed in a glass of water, the **scion** from the philodendron should grow roots in a few weeks.

   Ⓐ cutting
   Ⓑ leaf
   Ⓒ bud
   Ⓓ bloom

5. Suzanne was happy for the chance to **vindicate** her claim that she had discovered Mark Twain's diaries.

   Ⓐ promote
   Ⓑ publish
   Ⓒ prove
   Ⓓ withdraw

**Find an ANTONYM for each bold word. Then fill in the circle next to your answer.**

6. The 21st Amendment **rescinded** the 18th Amendment, thereby ending Prohibition.

   Ⓐ enforced
   Ⓑ ended
   Ⓒ cancelled
   Ⓓ annulled

7. The family **revered** their matriarch, and they came from the four corners of the globe to celebrate her 90th birthday with her.

   Ⓐ loved
   Ⓑ disrespected
   Ⓒ feared
   Ⓓ obeyed

8. The stranger was so **suave** that everybody was immediately put at ease.

Ⓐ rude

Ⓑ smooth

Ⓒ polite

Ⓓ pleasant

9. The artist's sketch was a **travesty** of what really happened at the rally.

Ⓐ approximation

Ⓑ imitation

Ⓒ distortion

Ⓓ facsimile

10. The **sordid** facts of the bribery scandal ruined the careers of all the people involved.

Ⓐ dirty

Ⓑ pleasant

Ⓒ offensive

Ⓓ disgusting

**Choose the best way to complete each sentence or answer each question. Then fill in the circle next to your answer.**

11. **Collusion** between businesses to artificially drive up demand for a product may be all of the following except

Ⓐ secret.

Ⓑ deceitful.

Ⓒ legal.

Ⓓ criminal.

12. **Indictments** involve what kind of charges?

Ⓐ civil

Ⓑ criminal

Ⓒ credit card

Ⓓ electrical

13. Which of the following does not have to do with **incinerating?**

Ⓐ recycling

Ⓑ burning

Ⓒ fire

Ⓓ ashes

14. The brothers' exchanges could be so **vitriolic** that strangers might think they hated each other. What element characterizes the exchanges?

Ⓐ jokes

Ⓑ flattery

Ⓒ bitterness

Ⓓ compliments

15. Which of the following is not **judicial?**

Ⓐ a judge

Ⓑ the courts

Ⓒ the law

Ⓓ a senator

## Standardized Test Preview/Practice

**In this passage, some of the words from this lesson are in bold. Read the passage and then answer the questions.**

**Judicial** interpreters are people fluent in at least two languages who help those who are **indicted** with a crime, and who don't speak English well, understand what is happening throughout the judicial process. These interpreters are highly

5 fluent in what is sometimes called "legalese"— the specialized language of the court.

Working with attorneys, judicial interpreters help individuals understand what is happening when they must stand before the judge to plead guilty or not guilty to a crime.

10 They must convey not just the meaning of the words spoken, but the tone as well—for example, when the tone from a sarcastic judge is **vitriolic.**

Judicial interpreters are always learning. Sometimes they are sent materials to study so they can become familiar with

15 specific technical words and phrases related to the evidence in a trial. An interpreter working on a case in which someone is indicted for setting a fire might have to learn the names of chemicals used for **incineration.** Or, if a case involves a religious group, the interpreter may need to learn about

20 beliefs, practices, and important religious figures such as **martyrs.**

1. In line 1, **judicial** means

   (A) court.

   (B) foreign.

   (C) working.

   (D) language.

2. The meaning of **indicted** (line 2) is

   (A) suspected of.

   (B) charged with.

   (C) fined for.

   (D) jailed for.

3. In line 12, **vitriolic** most nearly means

   (A) mean.

   (B) bitterly sarcastic.

   (C) extremely arrogant.

   (D) loud.

4. The word **incineration** (line 18) most nearly means

   (A) setting something on fire.

   (B) planning a crime.

   (C) putting out a fire.

   (D) putting someone in jail.

5. In line 21, **martyrs** means

   (A) religious educators.

   (B) leaders of churches.

   (C) those who have died for their beliefs.

   (D) lawyers involved in the case.

Name _____     Date _____

Lesson **20** **Test**

**Find a SYNONYM for each bold word. Then fill in the circle next to your answer.**

1. The letter looked to be from my long-lost uncle, but my mother suspected that it was **bogus.**

   Ⓐ overwhelming
   Ⓑ genuine
   Ⓒ friendly
   Ⓓ fake

2. The ascendancy of the automobile meant the **demise** of the horse-drawn buggy.

   Ⓐ revival
   Ⓑ end
   Ⓒ beginning
   Ⓓ decline

3. Sara **devised** a plan that would allow us to visit roadside attractions along our route from Florida to Washington.

   Ⓐ formed
   Ⓑ copied
   Ⓒ borrowed
   Ⓓ bought

4. News of Carl's delay **evinced** a frown from his grandfather.

   Ⓐ displayed
   Ⓑ expressed
   Ⓒ provoked
   Ⓓ demanded

5. Will was intimidated by the sheer weight of the **tome** assigned that week.

   Ⓐ experiment
   Ⓑ book
   Ⓒ essay
   Ⓓ problem

**Find an ANTONYM for each bold word. Then fill in the circle next to your answer.**

6. Not all decisions are **irrevocable.**

   Ⓐ permanent
   Ⓑ changeable
   Ⓒ correct
   Ⓓ unquestionable

7. **Martial** law was imposed in Hawaii after the bombing of Pearl Harbor.

   Ⓐ civil
   Ⓑ military
   Ⓒ wartime
   Ⓓ army

8. Taking pleasure in **mundane** details is key to happiness.

Ⓐ normal

Ⓑ usual

Ⓒ extraordinary

Ⓓ boring

9. Dawn **patronized** her older brother by reminding him to wear a coat and gloves.

Ⓐ insulted

Ⓑ condescended

Ⓒ belittled

Ⓓ respected

10. Several witnesses **refuted** her claim that she had never been in the restaurant before the robbery.

Ⓐ proved

Ⓑ supported

Ⓒ suggested

Ⓓ denied

**Choose the best way to complete each sentence or answer each question. Then fill in the circle next to your answer.**

11. A **quirk** of fate is most likely to be

Ⓐ sudden.

Ⓑ predictable.

Ⓒ unremarkable.

Ⓓ uninteresting.

12. The United States sometimes uses economic **sanctions** to try to influence policy in other countries. **Sanctions** are

Ⓐ problems.

Ⓑ unfair.

Ⓒ actions.

Ⓓ situations.

13. Which best describes an object that is **enshrined?**

Ⓐ dangerous

Ⓑ fragile

Ⓒ worthless

Ⓓ valued

14. Which of the following is least likely to be considered **memorabilia?**

Ⓐ a Beatles poster

Ⓑ an Eisenhower campaign button

Ⓒ today's newspaper

Ⓓ an old movie costume

15. A **querulous** person is most likely to

Ⓐ complain.

Ⓑ approve.

Ⓒ compliment.

Ⓓ flatter.

## Standardized Test Preview/Practice

**In this passage, some of the words from this lesson are in bold. Read the passage and then answer the questions.**

Jackson was excited. His stepmother, Shirley, was taking him to get his hair cut. Later that afternoon he would graduate from high school. He was glad he had Shirley to cheer him on today. There was nothing **bogus** about her. She'd become his
5  stepmother when he was just three years old, and she'd been there for him ever since. He had **enshrined** the memory of each time she'd picked him up after a long day of work at the hospital to give him a big hug. Even as a teenager, every time he felt alone or needed strength, all he had to do was think of
10  Shirley's hugs.

He was thrilled that Shirley had **sanctioned** his plans to get a stylish new haircut the morning of graduation. Jackson planned to get a fade and have his favorite barber, Mr. Lee, shave a geometric design on one side. He grinned when they
15  arrived at the barbershop they'd **patronized** for years. Jackson had learned a lot about life by talking to the regulars here. He even enjoyed listening to their **querulous** arguments because they made him think about current events in new ways.

As Mr. Lee began snipping Jackson's hair, he sighed. Today
20  was going to be amazing.

1. The meaning of **bogus** (line 4) is

   Ⓐ unpleasant.
   Ⓑ fake.
   Ⓒ sad.
   Ⓓ bad.

2. In line 6, **enshrined** means

   Ⓐ cherished.
   Ⓑ understood.
   Ⓒ liked.
   Ⓓ thought about.

3. The word **sanctioned** (line 11) most nearly means

   Ⓐ decided against.
   Ⓑ didn't allow.
   Ⓒ approved of.
   Ⓓ recommended.

4. The meaning of **patronized** (line 15) is

   Ⓐ put down.
   Ⓑ gone to.
   Ⓒ made fun of.
   Ⓓ passed by.

5. In line 17, **querulous** most nearly means

   Ⓐ critical.
   Ⓑ reasonable.
   Ⓒ constant.
   Ⓓ cruel.

**Lessons 1–20** **Final Test 1**

Read the passage. Choose the best answer for each sentence or question about a bold word. Then fill in the circle next to your answer.

# The Gabby Gorilla

Koko the gorilla, a **scion** of the San Francisco Zoo's breeding program, was named Hanabi-Ko, Japanese for "fireworks child," in honor of her birth on Independence Day in 1971. Life for Koko really became exciting a year later when she met Penny Patterson, a scientist who wanted to see if the great ape could communicate. Penny had learned of the work of other researchers who had taught sign language to chimpanzees, and she believed that gorillas had the same **potential.** Koko was an able student, with both the manual **dexterity** and intellectual **faculties** needed to express herself.

Koko's vocabulary has grown to more than 1,000 signs. She has used her hands to express everything from humor and emotion to insults and moral judgment. She even **articulates** her thoughts with some signs she invented herself. The language **prodigy** also understands some 2,000 spoken words. Although she is talented at communicating with her hands, Koko still uses her voice. Apparently purring and barking remain the best way to **enunciate** her pleasure and displeasure.

Her **maternal** side began to emerge when she told Penny she wanted a kitten. She chose a gray kitten and named him "All Ball." She **nurtured** the kitten like a mother would a baby gorilla, carrying him on her back and playing with him. When she lost All Ball to a traffic accident, the sadness she **evinced** showed that gorillas experience the same basic feelings as humans. Her fans all over the world felt tremendous **empathy** for her grief.

Koko has expressed her desire to **propagate,** but she has not become a mother. To improve the chances of Koko having a baby, Penny set up a form of video dating. She showed Koko videos of different male gorillas and let Koko decide which one she liked most. She chose Ndume, and the two are good friends. Penny and the zoo hope that Koko and her companion will one day become parents. One big question the researchers would like answered is whether Koko would **impart** her ability to communicate to her child. They have seen her shaping her doll's hands into signs, and they think she would probably pass that skill along to her young.

Even if Koko never becomes the mother of a line of talking apes, she has improved the public image of her species enormously. Before Koko, gorillas were thought to be stupid, vicious brutes incapable of intelligent thought or tender emotion. Since she learned to express herself in a way humans can understand, she has set the record straight.

1. In the first paragraph, **dexterity** refers to use of

    Ⓐ the head.

    Ⓑ the mouth.

    Ⓒ the legs.

    Ⓓ the hands.

2. What types of abilities are **faculties?**

    Ⓐ natural

    Ⓑ learned

    Ⓒ taught

    Ⓓ unusual

3. As used in the second paragraph, a SYNONYM for **articulates** is

    Ⓐ says.

    Ⓑ expresses.

    Ⓒ writes.

    Ⓓ implies.

4. Like Koko, a **prodigy** is

    Ⓐ extraordinary.

    Ⓑ childish.

    Ⓒ common.

    Ⓓ young.

5. A SYNONYM for **maternal** is

    Ⓐ playful.

    Ⓑ motherly.

    Ⓒ caring.

    Ⓓ selfish.

6. As used in the third paragraph, **nurtured** means

    Ⓐ cared for.

    Ⓑ abandoned.

    Ⓒ watched.

    Ⓓ raised.

7. A SYNONYM for **empathy** is

   Ⓐ feeling.

   Ⓑ sorrow.

   Ⓒ understanding.

   Ⓓ frustration.

8. As used in the fourth paragraph, **propagate** means

   Ⓐ reproduce.

   Ⓑ adopt.

   Ⓒ grow.

   Ⓓ change.

9. An ANTONYM for **evinced** is

   Ⓐ displayed.

   Ⓑ showed.

   Ⓒ hid.

   Ⓓ expressed.

10. Which is NOT a SYNONYM for **impart?**

    Ⓐ give

    Ⓑ bestow

    Ⓒ remove

    Ⓓ convey

## Standardized Test Preview/Practice

1. In the first paragraph, **scion** most nearly means

   Ⓐ resident.

   Ⓑ graduate.

   Ⓒ celebrity.

   Ⓓ favorite.

   Ⓔ descendant.

2. In the first paragraph, **potential** most nearly means

   Ⓐ intelligence.

   Ⓑ capacity.

   Ⓒ desire.

   Ⓓ talent.

   Ⓔ ability.

3. What best captures the meaning of the word **enunciate** in the second paragraph?

   Ⓐ describe

   Ⓑ suggest

   Ⓒ imply

   Ⓓ announce

   Ⓔ say

4. In the third paragraph, **evinced** most nearly means

   Ⓐ expressed.

   Ⓑ felt.

   Ⓒ experienced.

   Ⓓ seemed.

   Ⓔ withheld.

5. In the fourth paragraph, **impart** most nearly means

   Ⓐ demonstrate.

   Ⓑ bestow.

   Ⓒ show.

   Ⓓ explain.

   Ⓔ take.

## Final Test 2

**Read the passage. Choose the best answer for each sentence or question about a bold word. Then fill in the circle next to your answer.**

# The Prince of Peanuts

In the early 1800s, cotton was the main cash crop in the southern United States. The textile industry had strong demand for the plant, which thrived in the rich soil and warm climate. Over time, constant planting of the same crop **depreciated** the nutrients in the soil. Weaker soil led to weaker crops, which led to weaker profits. By the turn of the century, southern farmers faced economic disaster. Finding the solution to a problem often requires just thinking about the problem differently. Luckily for those farmers, an agricultural scientist at the time made it his **crusade** to find out how to sell what would grow, rather than how to grow what would sell.

George Washington Carver was born **enslaved** in Missouri during the Civil War. He showed a **precocious** talent for gardening and as a boy he was known as the "plant doctor" to friends and neighbors. He was eager to learn, but there were no local schools for African American students. His drive for **erudition** led him to Kansas, where he graduated from high school, and then to Iowa, where he went to college to study painting and piano. His talent with plants caught the attention of the Iowa State College Department of Horticulture, where he soon was the first African American student. He graduated in 1894 and became the first African American member of the Iowa State's faculty that year. He gained national attention studying plant **blights,** and he was invited to join the faculty at Alabama's Tuskegee Institute when he finished his master's degree in 1896.

He knew that the **antecedent** cause of the poor soil was constant planting of cotton, which demanded nitrogen from the soil. He knew that the land needed to take a break from cotton and to grow crops that restored nitrogen, like peanuts and soybeans. He also knew that there was no demand for peanuts and soybeans. His **sagacious** solution was to create demand. He spent the rest of his career developing a **multitude** of products from the **array** of crops best suited to the area. He created hundreds of products from local crops, including adhesives, cheese, ink, paper, and shaving cream. It is a **fallacy** that Dr. Carver invented peanut butter, although he did come up with more than 300 uses for the peanut.

His work had fast, **tangible** results. Peanuts became one of the country's leading crops and created an industry worth $200 million before 1940. Of all his hundreds of discoveries, he only patented three. He **contended** that his purpose was to help the people of the community, not to profit from them. When he died in 1943, he left his life's savings to the Tuskegee Institute so that his work could continue. Southern farmers still grow cotton, but thanks to Dr. Carver's work and legacy, they no longer depend on it.

1. **Precocious** people show their abilities when they are

   (A) old.

   (B) relaxing.

   (C) young.

   (D) under pressure.

2. In the second paragraph, **blights** means

   (A) seeds.

   (B) diseases.

   (C) blooms.

   (D) roots.

3. What is a problem's **antecedent?**

   (A) its cause

   (B) its solution

   (C) its result

   (D) its complication

4. In the third paragraph, **sagacious** means

   (A) bold.

   (B) risky.

   (C) clever.

   (D) wise.

5. In this passage, **multitude** describes

   (A) a large number of products.

   (B) a small number of products.

   (C) a stockpile of products.

   (D) a demand for products.

6. A SYNONYM for **array** is

   (A) a few.

   (B) a lot.

   (C) a sample.

   (D) a collection.

7. In the fourth paragraph, **contended** means

Ⓐ accepted.

Ⓑ disagreed.

Ⓒ disputed.

Ⓓ maintained.

8. An ANTONYM for **erudition** is

Ⓐ wisdom.

Ⓑ ignorance.

Ⓒ silliness.

Ⓓ importance.

9. A **crusade** takes place over what period of time?

Ⓐ instantly

Ⓑ a little while

Ⓒ a long time

Ⓓ forever

10. The **tangible** nature of Dr. Carver's work means the results could be

Ⓐ touched.

Ⓑ seen.

Ⓒ guessed at.

Ⓓ deduced.

## Standardized Test Preview/Practice

1. When something is **depreciated,** its value

   Ⓐ increases.

   Ⓑ doubles.

   Ⓒ decreases.

   Ⓓ ages.

   Ⓔ vanishes.

2. In the first paragraph, **crusade** most nearly means

   Ⓐ struggle.

   Ⓑ wish.

   Ⓒ command.

   Ⓓ hope.

   Ⓔ search.

3. What best captures the meaning of the word **erudition** in the second paragraph?

   Ⓐ freedom

   Ⓑ knowledge

   Ⓒ wealth

   Ⓓ power

   Ⓔ status

4. In the third paragraph, **fallacy** most nearly means

   Ⓐ given.

   Ⓑ victory.

   Ⓒ fact.

   Ⓓ secret.

   Ⓔ wrong idea.

5. In the fourth paragraph, **tangible** most nearly means

   Ⓐ radical.

   Ⓑ significant.

   Ⓒ destructive.

   Ⓓ real.

   Ⓔ unimportant.

## Final Test 3

Read the passage. Choose the best answer for each sentence or question about a bold word. Then fill in the circle next to your answer.

# Easy Come, Easy Go

Andrew Carnegie lived the American Dream. Born in Scotland in 1835, Carnegie and his family struggled as machines took the place of skilled labor in weaving, which was his father's trade. They came to America and settled in Pennsylvania when Carnegie was a teenager, and he soon found work in the railroad industry. He was already a rich man at 37 years old when he learned of a method for making the large quantities of steel the modern world was demanding. With wealth earned from making steel, he was able to give the world much more than building materials.

Carnegie's partner in the steel business, Henry Clay Frick, was interested in profits as well as power. He believed in running his business the way he wanted and felt that the factory workers had no right to a say in the matter. On the other hand, Carnegie had written essays in which he supported the right of workers to form unions to protect their own interests. Frick's normal response to pressure from unions was to absolutely refuse to **concede** their demands. Carnegie was interested in keeping the steel moving, and during one dispute with labor, he issued Frick an **injunction** to grant the union its demands and get the workers back to the factory.

Never **complacent,** Carnegie was always looking for better ways to do things. He wanted equipment of the highest **caliber,** on the cutting edge of technology. Better machines meant fewer employees were needed, but the strong unions prevented the company from letting anyone go. This time, Carnegie told Frick to handle it however he thought best, but not to give in. Carnegie and Frick wanted to do away with the union and **subjugate** its workers. The workers not only walked out, but they also tried to stop the factory from operating with replacements. Armed guards were brought in to protect the replacement workers, and a long, violent battle resulted. In the end, the state military had to step in to return control of the factory to its owners. Carnegie had won the fight, but the damage to his reputation as a champion for labor was done.

He did not want to be known as the man who went back on his word and betrayed the working class. In his later years, he focused his energy and fortune on making the world a better place. He wanted to achieve world peace, and **subsidized** those institutions he felt would advance that goal. The legacy of his philanthropy is **manifest** in the universities, libraries, hospitals, parks, and concert halls that bear his name.

Though he donated funds for nearly 3,000 libraries, his most notable gift may be a performance hall in New York City. Carnegie Hall opened its doors in 1891 and has hosted the world's **virtuoso** musicians for more than a century. A performance at Carnegie Hall is considered by many to be the **zenith** of a career in the performing arts. Some of his other donations were considered **eccentric** even by those that received them. In 1904, on a tour of Princeton University's athletic facilities, he had an idea. He decided that Princeton needed a lake where students could row to take their minds off of football, a sport of which he disapproved. Two years later, there was a three-mile lake at Princeton.

By the time he died in 1919, he had given away more than $350 million. Since then, the organizations he founded have given away over $2 billion. A **quirk** in his nature was that he disapproved of stockpiling wealth, yet he was the richest man of his time. He had a gift for gathering money, but it was balanced by the gifts he gave from it.

1. To **concede** to labor's demands, Frick would have

   Ⓐ ignored them.

   Ⓑ granted them.

   Ⓒ negotiated over them.

   Ⓓ denied them.

2. In the third paragraph, **caliber** means

   Ⓐ excellence.

   Ⓑ expense.

   Ⓒ value.

   Ⓓ rarity.

3. An ANTONYM for **subjugate** is

   Ⓐ liberate.

   Ⓑ enslave.

   Ⓒ empower.

   Ⓓ subdue.

4. A SYNONYM for **subsidize** is

   Ⓐ authorize.

   Ⓑ finance.

   Ⓒ plan.

   Ⓓ organize.

5. In this passage, **virtuoso** describes

   Ⓐ the most.

   Ⓑ the least.

   Ⓒ the best.

   Ⓓ the worst.

6. A SYNONYM for **zenith** is

Ⓐ edge.

Ⓑ bottom.

Ⓒ middle.

Ⓓ top.

7. In the fifth paragraph, **eccentric** means

Ⓐ odd.

Ⓑ ordinary.

Ⓒ generous.

Ⓓ unpredictable.

8. An ANTONYM for **complacent** is

Ⓐ dissatisfied.

Ⓑ happy.

Ⓒ content.

Ⓓ curious.

9. Which is NOT a SYNONYM for **manifest?**

Ⓐ apparent

Ⓑ visible

Ⓒ suggested

Ⓓ evinced

10. An ANTONYM for **injunction** is

Ⓐ order.

Ⓑ demand.

Ⓒ request.

Ⓓ idyll.

## Standardized Test Preview/Practice

1. In the second paragraph, **injunction** most nearly means

   Ⓐ suggestion.

   Ⓑ command.

   Ⓒ threat.

   Ⓓ urge.

   Ⓔ plea.

2. In the third paragraph, **complacent** most nearly means

   Ⓐ restless.

   Ⓑ calm.

   Ⓒ worried.

   Ⓓ satisfied.

   Ⓔ anxious.

3. What best captures the meaning of the word **manifest** in the fourth paragraph?

   Ⓐ evident

   Ⓑ hidden

   Ⓒ suggested

   Ⓓ implied

   Ⓔ alive

4. In the fifth paragraph, **zenith** most nearly means

   Ⓐ low point.

   Ⓑ beginning.

   Ⓒ end.

   Ⓓ highlight.

   Ⓔ peak.

5. In the sixth paragraph, **quirk** most nearly means

   Ⓐ peculiarity.

   Ⓑ defect.

   Ⓒ charm.

   Ⓓ element.

   Ⓔ aspect.

Name _____ Date _____

## Final Test 4

Read the passage. Choose the best answer for each sentence or question about a bold word. Then fill in the circle next to your answer.

# Form over Fashion

A uniform is an outfit that identifies its wearer as a member of a certain group. Police officers, package carriers, and flight attendants all wear the **garb** of their professions as a signal to the public about who they are and what can be expected of them. But not only do uniforms tell group outsiders something about group insiders, they also serve important functions within the groups. On the field of play and on the field of battle, it is crucial to be able to distinguish friend from foe. Off the field, a uniform is a boost to morale for the group that wears it. These are the primary functions for sports and military uniforms alike.

Modern military uniforms evolved as wealthy, powerful nations began to build standing armies. The **impetus** behind the decision to dress **militants** alike was as much to display that wealth and power as it was to protect and uplift the wearer. By the late 18th century, some of the world's armies wore sleeves tight enough to **impair** their musket aim and sword exercises, just for the sake of looking impressive.

The young American Revolutionary Army was much more practical. It asked that its soldiers wear a certain style of clothing, which included common things they probably already owned. They wore hunting shirts and their coats were usually brown, which was the most common color of clothing produced in the American Colonies at the time. But not having the right clothes was not a big problem, and if they needed to, they would wear whatever was available to them.

Revolutionary soldiers wore the design or color of their units on their hats. Like modern uniforms, the function of those hats was to identify members of the group. Hats were the hardest articles to come by and also the biggest source of a soldier's pride. Officers added certain **flamboyant** touches to their hats, such as feathers or buttons. These touches soon became incorporated as part of the officially **sanctioned** uniform to signify the wearer's rank and position.

The Quartermaster Corps was established on June 16, 1775, the same day that George Washington took over as Commander in Chief of the Revolutionary Army. A quartermaster is the supply officer, and is responsible for the army's food, clothing, and equipment. The quartermaster's responsibility includes uniforms. In 1779, Congress gave the Commander in Chief the authority to decide exactly how the Army should be uniformed. Things the Army wears and the ways in which it wears them has become a very complicated matter since then. The quartermaster now issues newly **inducted** soldiers everything they will need, from underwear to overcoats.

There are **myriad** shoes, hats, and everything in between that are acceptable to the army. They must be worn in specific combinations depending on the job, location, and occasion if the soldier is to **adhere** to the dress code. The details are very precise;

it takes more than 300 pages of instructions to cover all the rules. The army considers appearance to be an indication of discipline among its soldiers, and it takes the dress code seriously. Inspecting officers subject their **subordinates** to intense **scrutiny** and **censure** those who fail to meet standards.

Modern military uniforms emphasize functionality. Today's soldiers may be called upon to serve in any climate on Earth, and their clothing needs to provide the best comfort and protection possible. Soldiers in the desert, the jungle, the tropics, the Arctic, the city, and the country may look different. But the pride they feel when wearing their uniforms is the same.

1. The **militants** in the second paragraph were

   Ⓐ statesmen.
   Ⓑ fighters.
   Ⓒ poets.
   Ⓓ royalty.

2. An ANTONYM for **impair** is

   Ⓐ weaken.
   Ⓑ maintain.
   Ⓒ improve.
   Ⓓ lessen.

3. As used in the fourth paragraph, a SYNONYM for **sanctioned** is

   Ⓐ copied.
   Ⓑ tolerated.
   Ⓒ forbidden.
   Ⓓ approved.

4. When soldiers are **inducted,** they are

   Ⓐ admitted to service.
   Ⓑ banned from service.
   Ⓒ persuaded against service.
   Ⓓ forced into service.

5. In this passage, **adhere** means

   Ⓐ to ignore.
   Ⓑ to follow.
   Ⓒ to consider.
   Ⓓ to defy.

6. As used in the sixth paragraph, **subordinates**

Ⓐ are under someone else's command.

Ⓑ are free to do as they please.

Ⓒ answer to no one.

Ⓓ give orders.

7. A SYNONYM for **censure** is

Ⓐ to reward.

Ⓑ to find fault.

Ⓒ to praise.

Ⓓ to disappoint.

8. Which is NOT a SYNONYM for **garb?**

Ⓐ style

Ⓑ fabric

Ⓒ costume

Ⓓ outfit

9. An **impetus** is

Ⓐ the cause of something.

Ⓑ the result of something.

Ⓒ the idea of something.

Ⓓ the story of something.

10. An ANTONYM for **myriad** is

Ⓐ certain.

Ⓑ unlimited.

Ⓒ boundless.

Ⓓ few.

## Standardized Test Preview/Practice

1. In the first paragraph, **garb** most nearly means

   Ⓐ clothing.

   Ⓑ badge.

   Ⓒ color.

   Ⓓ haircut.

   Ⓔ trend.

2. In the second paragraph, **impetus** most nearly means

   Ⓐ excuse.

   Ⓑ history.

   Ⓒ driving force.

   Ⓓ logic.

   Ⓔ inspiration.

3. What best captures the meaning of the word **flamboyant** in the fourth paragraph?

   Ⓐ important

   Ⓑ impressive

   Ⓒ colorful

   Ⓓ showy

   Ⓔ frivolous

4. In the sixth paragraph, **myriad** most nearly means

   Ⓐ various.

   Ⓑ many.

   Ⓒ few.

   Ⓓ scarce.

   Ⓔ specific.

5. In the sixth paragraph, **scrutiny** most nearly means

   Ⓐ examination.

   Ⓑ glances.

   Ⓒ standards.

   Ⓓ norms.

   Ⓔ tests.

## Test Answer Key

### Lesson 1 Test

1. B
2. A
3. C
4. A
5. A
6. D
7. A
8. B
9. D
10. C
11. C
12. A
13. C
14. A
15. C

**STP/P**

1. C
2. A
3. C
4. D
5. B

### Lesson 2 Test

1. D
2. C
3. A
4. A
5. D
6. C
7. A
8. B
9. D
10. D
11. A
12. D
13. B
14. A
15. C

**STP/P**

1. A
2. C
3. D
4. C
5. A

### Lesson 3 Test

1. D
2. A
3. C
4. C
5. D
6. A
7. A
8. C
9. B
10. B
11. D
12. A
13. C
14. D
15. A

**STP/P**

1. A
2. B
3. C
4. A
5. B

### Lesson 4 Test

1. D
2. A
3. D
4. C
5. B
6. D
7. A
8. C
9. A
10. B
11. C
12. A
13. A
14. A
15. C

**STP/P**

1. C
2. B
3. C
4. A
5. B

### Lesson 5 Test

1. D
2. C
3. A
4. B
5. D
6. A
7. D
8. C
9. A
10. A
11. B
12. A
13. D
14. C
15. A

**STP/P**

1. A
2. B
3. C
4. D
5. B

### Lesson 6 Test

1. B
2. A
3. B
4. A
5. D
6. B
7. C
8. C
9. B
10. A
11. C
12. C
13. A
14. B
15. A

**STP/P**

1. B
2. A
3. C
4. B
5. B

### Lesson 7 Test

1. B
2. D
3. A
4. D
5. A
6. A
7. A
8. D
9. D
10. B
11. A
12. A
13. B
14. C
15. C

**STP/P**

1. A
2. C
3. B
4. D
5. C

### Lesson 8 Test

1. C
2. A
3. D
4. A
5. B
6. B
7. B
8. A
9. D
10. A
11. D
12. C
13 A
14. C
15. B

**STP/P**

1. C
2. C
3. D
4. B
5. A

## Lesson 9 Test

1. D
2. A
3. B
4. A
5. D
6. D
7. B
8. A
9. D
10. B
11. C
12. C
13. A
14. B
15. D

### STP/P

1. B
2. A
3. C
4. B
5. C

## Lesson 10 Test

1. C
2. A
3. D
4. A
5. B
6. B
7. C
8. C
9. A
10. B
11. C
12. B
13. D
14. C
15. A

### STP/P

1. D
2. B
3. C
4. C
5. A

## Midterm Test 1 (Lessons 1–10)

1. A
2. D
3. B
4. C
5. A
6. D
7. C
8. A
9. B
10. D

### STP/P

1. A
2. D
3. B
4. A
5. E

## Midterm Test 2 (Lessons 1–10)

1. C
2. D
3. A
4. D
5. B
6. A
7. C
8. D
9. A
10. B

### STP/P

1. C
2. B
3. E
4. B
5. A

## Lesson 11 Test

1. C
2. A
3. D
4. A
5. B
6. A
7. D
8. B
9. A
10. C
11. D
12. A
13. C
14. B
15. B

### STP/P

1. B
2. C
3. B
4. A
5. C

## Lesson 12 Test

1. B
2. A
3. D
4. B
5. A
6. C
7. D
8. A
9. D
10. C
11. B
12. A
13. A
14. A
15. C

### STP/P

1. B
2. A
3. C
4. A
5. B

## Lesson 13 Test

1. C
2. A
3. B
4. C
5. A
6. C
7. A
8. D
9. B
10. A
11. A
12. D
13. C
14. D
15. A

### STP/P

1. C
2. A
3. B
4. C
5. D

## Lesson 14 Test

1. A
2. B
3. D
4. A
5. C
6. B
7. A
8. B
9. D
10. C
11. B
12. D
13. D
14. B
15. B

### STP/P

1. C
2. A
3. C
4. B
5. C

## Lesson 15 Test

1. B
2. A
3. A
4. D
5. B
6. B
7. A
8. C
9. D
10. B
11. C
12. B
13. A
14. D
15. D

### STP/P

1. C
2. B
3. C
4. A
5. D

## Lesson 16 Test

1. B
2. A
3. C
4. D
5. C
6. B
7. C
8. B
9. A
10. D
11. C
12. B
13. A
14. A
15. D

### STP/P

1. A
2. B
3. D
4. C
5. A

## Lesson 17 Test

1. D
2. B
3. C
4. A
5. B
6. B
7. D
8. A
9. C
10. A
11. A
12. B
13. C
14. C
15. A

### STP/P

1. B
2. B
3. C
4. A
5. C

## Lesson 18 Test

1. A
2. B
3. B
4. A
5. D
6. A
7. C
8. B
9. C
10. B
11. C
12. D
13. B
14. A
15. A

### STP/P

1. C
2. A
3. C
4. B
5. A

## Lesson 19 Test

1. C
2. C
3. B
4. A
5. C
6. A
7. B
8. A
9. D
10. B
11. C
12. B
13. A
14. C
15. D

### STP/P

1. A
2. B
3. B
4. A
5. C

## Lesson 20 Test

1. D
2. B
3. A
4. C
5. B
6. B
7. A
8. C
9. D
10. A
11. A
12. C
13. D
14. C
15. A

### STP/P

1. B
2. A
3. C
4. B
5. A

## Final Test 1
## (Lessons 1–20)

1. D
2. A
3. B
4. A
5. B
6. A
7. C
8. A
9. C
10. C

### STP/P

1. E
2. B
3. D
4. A
5. B

## Final Test 2
## (Lessons 1–20)

1. C
2. B
3. A
4. D
5. A
6. B
7. D
8. B
9. C
10. A

### STP/P

1. C
2. A
3. B
4. E
5. D

# Final Test 3
## (Lessons 1–20)

1. B
2. A
3. A
4. B
5. C
6. D
7. A
8. A
9. C
10. C

## STP/P

1. B
2. D
3. A
4. E
5. A

# Final Test 4
## (Lessons 1–20)

1. B
2. C
3. D
4. A
5. B
6. A
7. B
8. B
9. A
10. D

## STP/P

1. A
2. C
3. D
4. B
5. A